TOO KIND

A Survival Guide for Sensitive Souls

ZEENAT AHMED-PETO

Too Kind: A Survival Guide for Sensitive Souls

Cover Designer and Typesetter: Neil Coe
Photography: Tia Talula
Editing: Precious Umurhurhu
Proofreading: Maudie Deiser Allotey
Logo Design: Tigz Rice
Logo Design Developer: Charlotte Raphael

First Edition: 2024
ISBN: 978-1-0686479-0-1

Published with the support of Brandspire Digital Limited, United Kingdom, https://brandspire.co.uk

Printed in the United Kingdom

DEDICATION

For Mum and Dad, for the solid foundation,
love and guidance.

And for Mothy and Hani, who have taught me
how to give and receive love.

ACKNOWLEDGEMENTS

I would like to thank Judith Lowe and PPD Learning Ltd for fostering my curiosity and Trevor Silvester and the Quest Institute for showing me what I could do with it.

A huge thank you goes out to my brothers who have supported me in countless ways throughout my life. Enormous thanks to my husband Hugh, who understands me and is my infinite cheerleader, always by my side.

Dr Liya Jacob, who awakened a dream in me, Hela Wozniak-Kay, Debbie Gilbert and the sisters at Sister Snog for the inspiration and, most especially, Mindy Gibbins-Klein for her expertise and support.

The people who have helped shape my ideas and have been supporters, new and old: Hugh Peto, Hasin Ahmed, Hasib Ahmed, Habiba Ahmed, Kirti Ahmed, Ammy Ahmed, Lucinda Blackett, Hani Peto, Sarah Schofield, Hayriye Mistiki, Julie Hinckley, Claire Oliveri, Hilias Ioannou, Emma-Louise Follows, Iain Hilleary, Charles Peto, Jacqueline Peto, Mahnaz Nazneen, Tasneen Khandaker, Talia Zamora, Tasnim Khan, Nahim Mahmood, Jo Permaul, Marie-Louise O'Neill and Ama Zaky.

Thank you so much to my beta readers, all of whom have helped shape this book.

And finally, infinite thanks to all of the clients I have worked with whose stories help me to help others.

CONTENTS

Chapter 11. You Can Love Yourself and Grow Unconditional Positive Self-Regard

Chapter 12: Bonus Exercises

INTRODUCTION

I have been practising cognitive hypnotherapy for over 10 years now and I have written this book as a response to the issues I work on with the clients I see regularly. They are interesting and resourceful professionals: high achievers who work hard and take care of others. They have a sensitive side where they feel things deeply and have a full life with many interests and ambitions. Yet, there is something that is holding them back from living their absolute dream life. They might find themselves at a crossroads, or maybe they want to change something about themselves, which has led them to where they are today. Many of my clients want to work on their self-esteem, their boundaries and their self-love. Others are working out where they stand in their relationship and whether to go into the next phase of life together or apart.

Most people I see will ask for help with something that is bothering them in their life *right now*. I know that mostly, what they are experiencing are *symptoms of a deeper issue*. A client might say that they are having trouble sleeping, experiencing pressure at work, struggling to maintain work-life balance, and are feeling a bit lost and disconnected in their relationship. They are unlikely to recognise the roots of their problems and how they could be related.

The stories I have drawn upon in this book are from people who have common underlying issues which can show up in low self-esteem, poor boundaries, and a commitment to pleasing others first, rather than themselves. In many cases, they have struggled with chronic illnesses or auto-immune disorders. However, despite having many tests to understand the cause of their symptoms, the results often come back negative. They report that the doctors couldn't find anything and yet; they continue to experience the symptoms. As Dr Brian Roet says, "…there are a proportion of symptoms which may be viewed as *messages* to be understood, rather than problems to be removed" (Roet. B, Hypnosis: A Gateway to Better Health, 1986).

This is often when they conclude that there may be a psychological connection, which leads them to seek help in the form of therapy. As Dr Gabor Mate says in The Myth of Normal, "There is nothing novel about the notion of the mind and body being intricately linked. If anything, what is new is the belief … that they are separable." (Mate. G, The Myth of Normal, 2023).

I have found time and again that when people are *too kind*; they are not kind to themselves. The niggling symptoms or recurrent aches and pains become louder and louder until they are heard. For some people, their bodies are screaming out in pain before they make the decision to do something about it and work out what's going on. If no medical reason for their symptoms can be found, then the root must be psychological, they reason. If there is no outlet for emotions to surface and be felt and experienced fully, they can simmer until they reach boiling point. In these cases, I find that once the emotional roots are addressed, feelings of anxiety – which are experienced as physical symptoms as well as a heightened emotional state, can start to reduce, as can other distressing emotions.

Through my work in clinical practice, I have built up a bank of examples of people who have chosen to improve their lot in life; they have chosen themselves. Understanding the reasons why they feel the need to constantly please others can help them to change these behaviours and create new, better ways of thinking and being.

The purpose of this book, then, is to share what I have learnt about how kind, sensitive people, can learn to love themselves and put their needs first sometimes.

My sincere wish is that my readers receive the underlying message: That creating happiness is a choice, and that it takes time and effort to learn to put yourself first. That it is the perfect time to challenge the messages that you have internalised over your lifetime: that looking after yourself and your needs is selfish.

In this book, I am sharing some of the tools to guide you to getting to know yourself better, and to use your sensitivity and kindness to love yourself as well as others.

You can be happy, too.

How to Use This Book

Each of the chapters of this book has their own stories within them and contains one or more exercises. I recommend that you complete the exercises using a pen and a journal or paper, as that is the best way to benefit from them. Take as much time as you need to complete the exercises, some of which can be done several times. All of the exercises are available on my website, where you can download the templates and fill them in if you prefer. I recommend reading this book in sequence, as the chapters have been laid out to follow on from one another. However, if you prefer, you can dip in and out of this book and just go to the sections which would be most useful. There are some clients whose stories are woven through several chapters, who you will get to know quite well, and others who I have cited briefly. It is not necessary to remember which client is which; the stories are given to illustrate a point. It is my belief that to have the greatest benefit, it would be useful to complete the exercises to the best of your ability.

NB: *All of the names and some of the details in this book have been changed to protect the identities and privacy of the people involved.*

To access the exercise templates and bonus materials, please visit:

https://zeenatahmedpeto.com/book-bonuses/

Enter the password: TooKindBonus!

"In the infinity of life, where I am, all is perfect,

whole and complete, and yet life is ever-changing.

There is no beginning and no end...

Life is never stuck or static or stale,

for each moment is ever new and fresh...

I rejoice in the knowledge that I have the power

of my own mind to use in any way that I choose.

Every moment of life is a new beginning point

As we move from the old. This moment is a new point

of beginning for me right here and right now.

All is well in my world."

Louise Hay, You Can Heal Your Life, 1984

CHAPTER 1

You Deserve to Be Happy

You have as much right to be happy as anybody else. The poem Desiderata says, 'You are a child of the universe no less than the trees and the stars; you have a right to be here'

(Ehrman. M, Desiderata, lines 22-23, 1927).

It may be that for some reason, you have not yet fully realised this in your life. This book will show you that you deserve to be happy and that it is okay for you to feel that you want more for yourself. Perhaps you have come to a point in your life where you are ready to take the steps to put yourself first for a change. This may feel uncomfortable and out of character, but in this book, you can learn how to do that, while remaining considerate and thoughtful. You can be happy, too.

Why do some people find it difficult to put themselves first and fulfil their own happiness? In this book, I will share examples of numerous clients from my cognitive hypnotherapy practise. Many of them have expressed that they have been told directly that they should put others' needs first; that it is righteous to be a martyr or to 'turn the other cheek'. The cultural expectations in the family of origin of my clients have often played an important role in the way they have formed their ideas in early childhood.

Perhaps they have heard comments or discussions from their earliest days about the virtues of being kind and thoughtful towards others. Men and women from generations gone by have certainly had the responsibility on their shoulders to work hard and support their families from a young age. Their happiness or desires often didn't come into it; the emphasis was on working hard for the greater good of the family and their community.

The first client we will meet is David, who grew up watching his father work very hard, always putting the welfare of his family first. After long hours at work, his father would help around the house, to ease the burden on his wife. This, David acknowledged, was unusual for the time. As a young man growing up, David internalised the beliefs that it is important to be kind and to look after one's family, just like his father before him. With his desire to help, over time, he has taken responsibility for more and more household chores and now finds himself completely exhausted after a long day at work. He regularly volunteers to help his wife, children, friends, parents, colleagues and boss. As he takes on more, it seems they take on less. His elderly parents are needing more care as their collective health is declining, and his wife is gripped by anxiety and bouts of depression, which means that he has to shoulder more than his share of the responsibilities.

David is constantly trying to please the other people in his life and yet, he has ended up feeling resentful. He is irritated by his brother's apparent lack of care towards their parents and feels he has to do the brunt of the work. David has lost all sense of himself, as he doesn't have the time or energy to do anything for his own leisure. "Why do I keep doing this?" David asks himself in my therapy room. He mentions that he has been putting other people first for as long as he can remember.

My opening sentence was "You have as much right to be happy as anyone else" – but there is a flaw in that statement. This is because we have a perception of how happy other people are and the reality is not always what it seems. From the outside, David has a life of great success in the material sense and in his professional life. But this belies a life of personal struggle. Despite looking accomplished and successful, he has struggled in his relationships for many years, his whole life, in fact. As I described, his father was his role model and somehow, whatever David does, he doesn't feel he matches up to that ideal. Underneath his attempts to help other people, there is a belief that *he just isn't good enough*. So he keeps trying harder.

When he embarked on therapy, David was at a crossroads. Although he was deeply unhappy, he decided that he couldn't make the changes that were needed to help him improve his situation. It would require breaking up his marriage, and he was not willing to do that, because of the impact it would have on his wife, children, and parents. David now realises that he and his wife didn't really 'choose' each other; it was more that they were both just there. It wasn't a romantic beginning, but more of a practical one and now, looking back, he can see that it set the tone for the whole marriage.

David knew that his need to help others was so strong that it stopped him from making better choices for himself in his own life. It's almost like the positive feelings he received from helping his friends and family were stronger than his love for himself. This is why he continued to put other people's wishes and desires in front of his own.

By talking through his feelings, David was able to bring back some semblance of control and make improvements in his day-to-day life. He started off by giving himself things to look forward to and savour. He was able to create some enjoyment for himself, more awareness and even gratitude for parts of his current situation.

Like many of my male therapy clients, David doesn't often share his burdens or fears with anyone else. We don't really know what other people are going through unless they tell us directly, and even then, it may be couched in a way that doesn't give us the whole truth, perhaps to spare *our* feelings.

The truth is, when you're happy, you can give your best. Happiness and a sense of being happy are infectious, and like so many other emotions, it can spread from one person to another. There is a virtuous circle of 'choosing to act happy' and then continuing the cycle of 'being happy' by behaving in the way a happy person would. By behaving in this way, and *choosing to have happy thoughts*, our minds start to feel happier, too.

When I was a primary school teacher many years ago, I met a young child who seemed to frown most of the time. She appeared as though she was perpetually wronged. I tried to engage her in conversation, to find out what she liked to draw her in, but to no avail. A couple of weeks went by with this new child in my class, and I decided to talk about emotions we experience. We sat in a circle and passed around a mirror, looking at our faces and making a wide range of expressions in response to jokes or funny stories. When the mirror reached the child in question, she seemed surprised at her own lack of range of facial expressions. She slowly started to smile and laugh, looking at her peers, and found the whole exercise amusing and fun. Later that week, I met her mother and noticed that she also didn't show many facial expressions. So perhaps the child had not picked up the visual cues her brain was programmed to from her mother from birth – hence her lack of facial expressions and her difficulty both showing and reading others' emotions. Over time this little girl became a happy and cherished member of the class. She learnt how to see the emotions in others, pick them up and emulate them, which helped her to *feel* them. She was infected with happiness.

Self-Esteem and Happiness

Meet Christos. He decided to live apart from his wife, Eleni, as their relationship had become a constant string of arguments. The strain was evident in both of them. Eleni had become spiteful and vicious, and Christos' self-esteem was at rock bottom. Whatever he did was not good enough. The thought of their child being exposed to this bitterness and anger was very distressing to him. For years, there was constant conflict within him because he would agree, just to pacify Eleni, even though it pained him to do so. Christos knew that he was doing it to keep the peace, as he hated any kind of conflict. He embarked on therapy when he took the bold step of moving out to give the couple some space.

Christos spent time talking about his childhood and he examined the roots of his fear of disagreeing with his wife. Why was he so afraid to share *his* point of view? Christos realised that he had a deep fear that he would not be loved if he didn't agree with her – or with anyone, for that matter. His unconscious mind had internalised the idea that he would only be loved if he did what other people wanted.

The Virtuous Circle

Some six months after separating, Christos has seen much improvement in his relationship. He is much happier since he took the hard step of moving out and he has changed some of his behaviours and the unsaid rules of engagement with Eleni. Things have improved since he explained that he wanted to be shown more consideration and spoken to more fairly. This has interrupted the pattern of behaviour which had become the norm for many years, as he used to accept put-downs and poor conduct. This change has already begun to impact their relationship positively. As his self-esteem grows, Christos expects to be treated with the same respect that he affords his wife. He can see the positive effects of the virtuous cycle on his wife and child and the impact it's had on them because he is stronger and happier. This, in turn, has an impact on them, hence a virtuous circle.

Christos came to realise that he had always been so concerned about other peoples' feelings, that he allowed them to speak to him in ways that most of us would find unacceptable: talking down to him, being rude, putting him down, and taking advantage of his kindness. He started to feel like a push-over and he hated that. He realised it wasn't worth being liked by others if he didn't like himself. Poor boundaries were something Christos had experienced throughout his life. When we started working together, he was fed-up with his inability to say no, or to stand up for himself. He avoided conflict at all costs, even with his employees. He would just let things go, rather than have an uncomfortable conversation. When we traced it back, it became obvious that these were a set of learnt ways of thinking, beliefs which had been instilled in him since childhood. Christos was encouraged to show respect to others, including his elders, and even his siblings. Being the eldest, this placed a responsibility on him to support the needs of everyone else in the family, and he became an expert at it. So much so, that when he met his first serious partner, Eleni, he was all set up for putting his needs aside and constantly trying to fulfil hers. His mind was primed for this unconsciously, and so they built their relationship this way, with him doing everything and anything Eleni wanted, often at his own cost. Now, in the present day, he has chosen to change all of this and create more balance in his life.

As he started to unpick the roots of this behaviour, he was able to challenge those patterns. He acknowledged how bad he felt when he let people walk all over him, and this increased his desire for self-respect. We worked on his conscious behaviours and the unconscious beliefs and values underpinning them, through conversational coaching, therapy and hypnosis. At each weekly session, we tracked his progress and drew out examples of where he felt more resilient and robust. Over time, his confidence grew in different areas of his life, as he started to find his voice once more, something which he hadn't accessed fully since he was very young. Christos emerged as a stronger, more self-assured version of himself, someone with healthy boundaries, who knew how to ask for what he wanted, as he had grown so much and had a new-found respect for himself.

Since he has taken these steps, Christos has reported huge positive changes in all areas of his life. He attributes this to the way he has changed his own behaviour and the conduct he will accept from other people. Improving his boundaries in his personal life has positively impacted how he conducts himself in his business, too. Christos has also been sharing his natural kindness in different ways, as he likes to help and support people in any way he can. He has recognised that he can touch people's lives by being a great dad, a godfather to his godchild, and by mentoring his employees, whilst maintaining his self-respect.

Being Happy Means You Can Give Your Best

When you are happy and content within yourself, you can do your best work and share your best ideas with other people. I met Hiba, a counsellor who supports people with eating disorders and has personal experience of this condition. She came to London as a child refugee. Having grown up in a camp until then, she and her family had faced great adversity and hardship. Arriving in London aged nine to a place of abundance had a huge impact on her in her formative years. Hiba described to me the numerous sacrifices she had to make for other family members while she was growing up. There was very little money around and she faced many challenges starting school in a new country. Giving and caring for her younger siblings was part of Hiba's earliest memories, and as such, she found it hard to speak up or say no to requests. The challenging circumstances of her childhood had adverse effects on how she felt about herself: like a person perpetually out of place. Over time, this became a way to punish herself – to put herself last and demonstrate her self-loathing, while indulging in over-eating when she had the opportunity. Eating comfort foods is known to dampen down feelings of anxiety for many people, and once a person has experienced periods of starvation, it makes sense that eating to excess could become a habit to create a sense of safety.

As the years went on, Hiba developed binge eating disorders and rapidly put on excess weight. She tried every diet and nutritional plan under the sun, but she couldn't keep off the weight she lost. Over time, this became hazardous to her health, and Hiba eventually decided to opt for bariatric surgery to help her to lose weight once and for all.

Although the surgery was successful, she reports that the psychological support was sadly lacking. Her body had changed, but her mind was still running the same programmes of fear and mistrust that there wouldn't be enough food. Hiba started to worry that she might undo all of the sacrifices she had been through, as she still craved high-fat, high-sugar foods. It was through extensive therapy and counselling that she was able to come to terms with her past and update her unconscious mind to realise that she was safe and that she would not starve. She has worked hard on her self-esteem and has learnt that it's okay to say no, even though she has deep empathy for other people.

Nowadays, Hiba is able to help other people with eating disorders and aid their recovery, because she is happier than she has ever been. This means she can support others whilst being strong in herself. This sense of freedom in her own happiness, and feeling comfortable with who she is now, has allowed her to recognise a sense of purpose. There is a reason why she has been through all those challenges and dark times. Hiba feels her calling is now to help others, and she can, because she is happy herself.

Follow the Light

I believe every soul is sacred, and that means we all deserve to be happy. That includes me and you. In a way, it's *our job* to be happy. You have been given a life and your mission, should you choose to accept it, is to be happy. It sounds simplistic, but the journey isn't always that simple!

There was a time in my life when I was desperately unhappy, stricken with grief, with an aching body, having lost all sense of who I was and what I was doing. I had experienced what I now recognise to be burnout, as I was struggling with the demands of my teaching career, coinciding with the diagnosis of an auto-immune condition, which was exhausting. Each day was a struggle, even to get out of bed and go to work, but I continued to work hard, determined to be a great teacher. I tended to take on too much and to worry about other people's problems as if they were my own. My gift of empathy was slowly suffocating me. Determined to make a success of my life and absolutely *not fail*, I struggled on with a relationship that was no longer working, but in time it came to an abrupt end. While I was reeling from the shock of the breakdown of my marriage and was hibernating from the world at large, I started to see an image of a well in my mind's eye. It was a deep well. It was lonely and cold in the pit of the well, and I was searching around in the dark, for weeks and weeks. This image seemed to pop into my head regularly. I also had images of my auto-immune condition – both the disease in my cells and the illness – the way I experienced it. The images that came to mind were that of a rocky seabed, clumps of rocks connected together, strewn with seaweed, quite grotesque in parts, with the tide coming in and out, revealing more of the rocks at times. I also imagined my personal boundaries as a fishing net, which had become so worn that it was full of holes, letting everything through. I realised that I could manipulate these images. After all, my mind had created them! Having an auto-immune condition made me think about what was going on. My immune cells were turning on me, gallantly putting up a fight, but shooting own goals! I began to wonder whether since my body could make it, maybe my body could also fix it? Or maybe my mind, body and spirit could work together to make things better?

One day, after several months, I noticed a glimmer of light above me. I had to strive hard to drag myself out of the well, climbing up towards the light, until I eventually emerged, completely changed as a new version of myself. Now when I look back, I realise I discovered new lands, ones which I didn't even know existed. Back then, it was about surviving, one day at a time. I was simply thinking about getting through the day. But I believed we should all seek our own happiness and that we have a responsibility towards ourselves to *create* our own happiness. That's what occurred to me back then – that it was *my* responsibility, and that only I had the power to change things for myself. Yes, I had good people around me, people who loved and cared for me – close family members and good friends, but ultimately, I had to make the choice to seek my own happiness. I had to decide that that was what I was going to do for myself. No longer relying on someone else to provide me with the feelings of security I so desired, that instead had to come from within. I didn't realise that at the time, but I believe that is how I came back to living a life where I felt deep contentment and peace within.

What I experienced could be termed as post-traumatic growth (PTG), where a person can experience enormous growth by getting through the struggle of personal life challenges.

In these situations, people can feel better than they ever have, because they are reframing something challenging into a learning experience, where one can blossom (Reading. S, The Self-Care Revolution, 2017).

Being too kind to everyone but myself was not serving me. I had to choose to love myself and treat myself with respect and honour my desire to be happy.

Seeking Your Own Happiness

David, whom we met in Chapter 1, has been working through his decision to seek his own happiness. He has been feeling stuck and unsatisfied for a number of years, both in his work-life and in his marriage. Over time, he and his wife have drifted apart, and most of their communication has been about their children. Now that the children are almost fully grown, he no longer feels like an essential part of the equation. He can maintain and build his relationship with his sons, who are now old enough to visit him independently, wherever he might be. David has dreams of travelling, maybe living abroad, and trying new and exciting things. His wife Ellen doesn't share those dreams, and he realises now that she probably never has. They have lived their lives carefully, never straying far from home, and yet, he now feels an urge to go out and try something new. He is excited by the prospect of a new life. It has been difficult to get Ellen to communicate her wishes; she is afraid of what he will say. He wants changes, she wants to stay the same. David has always put Ellen's wishes first, doing whatever he thought she wanted. He now thinks he's been so thoughtful that he has not honoured his own wishes. At this point in his life, he is ready to ask for more.

Our levels of happiness, contentment, and feelings of peace change over time. Life has its ups and downs and, for some people, those ups and downs have been very dramatic at times. Here is an exercise you can try to map out an overview of your life.

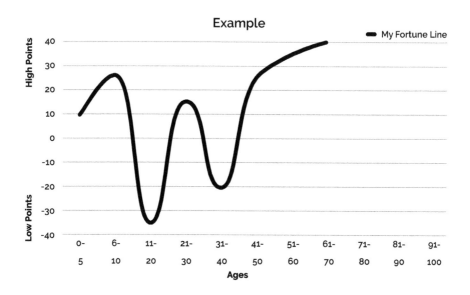

EXERCISE 1A:

Your Fortune Line

1. Download and print the blank template of the graph from: https://zeenatahmedpeto.com/book-bonuses/

2. Alternatively, draw two axes on a sheet of paper or in your journal. The x-axis should start across the middle of the page, and the y-axis should go from the top to the bottom of the page. The x-axis represents your age over time and the y-axis represents the highs and lows over your lifetime.

3. On a separate piece of paper write down the major events of your life – both the positive ones and the difficulties you've faced.

4. In brackets write the age you were at each of those events in time, e.g. (24).

5. Now space out your age over time along the x-axis – spread out the intervals as required. If you are using the template, it has been done for you.

6. Plot the major life events onto the graph with the two axes and draw a line to follow the events. The negative events can go into the negative part of the graph (below the x-axis).

7. Now your graph is complete, take time to look over it and consider the following questions, answering in a journal or on paper. Take as long as you need to explore the questions, which you could answer in one sitting or over a period of days.

EXERCISE 1B:

Our Fortune Line Journaling Questions:

1. At what period of your life were you most content and happy?

2. What helped create that period of contentment?

3. When you experienced the low points, what helped you to get back up to feeling stable and content?

4. What factors helped you maintain your positive feelings at good times in your life?

5. What is the common thread of what you absolutely *must have* to feel positive, content, and happy?

6. Imagine that you are at the highest point of the graph in the near future. What would your life be like if you were the most content you could be? Describe a whole day in that positive future state in as much detail as you can and entitle it 'A Day in My Dream Life'.

You've got one life, and it's up to you how you choose to lead it.

CHAPTER 2

You Can Change the Way You Think and Behave

We used to think that the brain was static, but now we know it is plastic, meaning that it can change and grow new neural networks (Cherry. K, What is neuroplasticity?, 2022). The neurons that fire when we repeat a thought over and over again, become fused together, so that this circuit becomes a closed loop. This means that decisions can be made on autopilot. These automatic thoughts require no thinking – so these reactions become unconscious. Now we understand, thanks to modern neuroscience, that it is possible to create new neural pathways – with some effort at the beginning. These new behaviours or thoughts need to be reinforced repeatedly, until they become a habit and go from conscious decisions to unconscious thoughts. This could be why we often hear that it takes 21 to 30 days to form a habit and up to 90 days to make it permanent. So, if you are starting a new exercise or health regime, you will need to repeat it daily until that new habit is formed. Over this time, the neurons in the brain's circuitry will wire together and fire together, making it just something you do every day, without having to think too much about it.

> In order to break a habit, you essentially want to disconnect the neurons which are currently connected. I have had lots of clients who habitually smoke at a certain time of day, or with a cup of coffee or even with certain people. Our brains make connections between all sorts of things, some of those are easy to spot and some of the connections are below the level of conscious awareness. That's where I am often looking to unhook connections by communicating with the unconscious mind in my work as a hypnotherapist. So this means that you can change how you think, even if it has been a habitual pattern throughout your life.

Three Timelines

Sometimes we forget all that we have been through because we are currently focussed on what's happening in the here and now. I often explain to my clients that we work together in three 'timelines' – meaning we talk about what is happening for them now, in the present, where that may have roots in their past and what they want to work towards in the future. Notice where your attention lies – are you present, past or future focussed? If you are struggling with a decision about something or you are at a crossroads, you may be looking back to the past quite a lot. This can be looking back with sadness or regret, and although it sounds negative, it can help you understand how you got to where you are today. This, in turn, can be a catalyst for what you want to create for your future reality.

Stages of Learning

The four stages of learning show that you can learn new processes and methods of thinking. At the start, there is a conscious decision involved, where you decide what you want instead of what you already have. In this case, it's the habits, behaviours and patterns of thinking that we are focussing on. Over time, and with ongoing practise this conscious competence can lead to unconscious competence. These new ways of being become just that – an automatic way of being.

Unconscious incompetence > Conscious incompetence > Conscious competence >Unconscious competence

The Conscious Competence Ladder was developed by Noel Burch in the 1970s. (Mindtools Content Team, The Conscious Competence Ladder, No Date) It's a useful model to understand how we go from not even knowing what we don't know, to becoming competent at something without any conscious effort. At first, you don't even know what you can't do, then you become aware of your lack of knowledge or skill, then with guidance and practise you learn how to do it well, with thinking and effort. Eventually, you can do it well with limited effort. This is what a successful therapy journey looks like, whether you work with a therapist or go on the personal development journey yourself.

Changing the Conversation

Zoe, a woman in her 30s, would often find herself ending up having frustrating conversations with her mother, where she felt they were going in circles. This client couldn't understand how these conversations kept starting again and again. She was unable to trace the arc of how they got from having a perfectly nice time to ending up in a dead-end conversation. These would inevitably lead to arguments, and she would find herself having to backtrack and say anything she could to pacify her mother who would back her into a corner with her arguments. This had gone on over her teenage years and into her 20s. When she reached her 30s, she decided to make this stop. By this time, Zoe had more control and was able to walk away more easily, as she had started to work on her boundaries in other parts of her life. So, every time one of these conversations started, and she could see where it was going, she would cut the conversation short and make an excuse to leave. This is known as a pattern interrupt, as it was changing the expected pattern of behaviour. She soon started to explain in a simple sentence, that she didn't want to continue this conversation as it wasn't enjoyable or productive and was making her feel unhappy. Over time, the incidence of these sorts of conversations diminished to being very rare. This had been a pattern these two people had been stuck in for decades, but with the decision and the effort to change it, their relationship improved overall, and now Zoe has stronger boundaries throughout her life.

Change Happens Naturally Over Time

Living in North London, I have grown up with many members of the community who came to this part of the world from their homes overseas in the 1960s, my own parents included. Many of those people held on to the beliefs they arrived with, and in fact were surprised when people in their country of origin were changing faster than them, in a bid to keep up with the modern world. This meant that many of them resisted change, consciously, especially if they hoped to maintain the nuances of their cultural beliefs and traditions so they could share them with their children and grandchildren.

However, over time and with experience, some of our collective views and ideas shift and adapt to the place and time in which we live; sometimes creating a set of hybrid beliefs and sub-cultures. So even with minimal effort and no conscious effort to change, we *cannot not* change. I certainly see that in the rich tapestry of cultures I meet in London where I live and work.

Behaviour is Learnt and You Can Learn a New Behaviour

We learn the majority of our behaviours in our formative years, which form a blueprint for how we do things, following what we see from our primary caregivers. We absorb these behaviours from what we are exposed to – what we see, hear and feel. It is said that we are the company we keep, and that the five people who we spend the most time with have the biggest impact on us. This means it is important to choose who we spend our time with, as much as possible. We have all heard of someone being a 'bad influence' on a teenager for example. This, of course, can carry on throughout life if we are susceptible to choosing the same 'bad influences' to spend time with.

It's often the case that people who drink to excess or take recreational drugs habitually, like to have someone to hang around with, someone who can join them and partake. When my clients are working on changing their habits, they often consider changing how they nurture these friendships. Often, when the activity of drinking together, for example, changes, it changes the quality of the friendship, as they no longer have that association in common.

Learning New Ways of Thinking and Behaving

Sophie had found herself in a series of unhappy relationships. When we met, she was trying to work out whether she could save her marriage which had rapidly gone downhill, since she found out that her husband was lying to her about numerous personal matters. Although she had spent many hours trying to justify his excuses to herself, she instinctively did not trust him anymore, as his stories just did not add up. Deep down, she knew he had been unfaithful. Sophie wanted desperately to believe him and for everything to be all right, but despite his lies, she was beginning to see more and more holes in the story.

She knew that her acceptance of his abusive behaviour was wrong; her friends had told her to leave, but she felt that somehow it was her fault. That her husband was angry because of something *she had done* to make him angry. Sophie had entered into therapy to improve her self-esteem, which was very low at the time. She realised that this pattern of behaviour was a familiar one, her previous partners had also been controlling and aggressive. Despite this, she knew that if she could find new ways to think, she would be able to behave differently, and her situation would change.

How we behave is linked to our beliefs, so during our sessions we traced back through Sophie's life to find that her life was echoing that of her parents. Her mother, like her, had been coerced and had become accustomed to pacifying a domineering and insecure husband, Sophie's father. She recognised the parallels between how her mother had accepted this as her lot and had always made excuses for her father. Sophie had grown up absorbing these attitudes and beliefs – it was easier and safer to be a people pleaser, and now she was re-creating the same situation in her own life. The unconscious mind had created a blueprint for her to follow and that's what she did, until something in her told her to interrupt that pattern and make a change.

Change is Possible

When you are in the throes of making changes, it can feel very turbulent and that can make you apprehensive about taking the next step. Most of my clients come to me at the point when they know change is coming and they want guidance to help them navigate through it. They are on the cusp of change, or are at a crisis point, having to choose the next path to take. Although only they can make those decisions, it can be helpful to have a guide walking alongside them.

Remember Christos from Chapter 1? He had come to that crossroads and had decided he could no longer be in an abusive relationship with his wife. His dilemma about leaving his wife concerned his child. By leaving the family home, it meant he would not be able to see his young daughter every day. Yet he decided it was the best thing for the family at that time, as it would reduce the clashes at home and give the couple time apart to take stock and work out where they would go from here.

Find Inspiration Within

Some years ago, a young woman named Simone came to see me to help her heal from a devastating break-up. At the time, she felt she was still so in love with her ex-partner, that it hit her extremely hard and what she experienced was akin to a bereavement. She later told me that getting through that break-up was one of the hardest things she had ever had to do. In this relationship, she was always on her toes, as the validity of her arguments or thoughts would be challenged constantly. At first, it was exciting having this level of intellectual conversation, although Simone thought she couldn't possibly be right because her partner was older and so much more educated and aware of the world. In time, she noticed the power struggle and how she was challenged, even over a personal preference. Simone had become so used to her partner winning the argument, that she gave up trying. Her boundaries became weaker and weaker until the time she started attending therapy sessions. At that point, she didn't really know what she thought about anything anymore.

Simone had been grieving the loss of her adoptive mother who had died a couple of years before and was also in the process of tracing her birth parents and exploring her roots and unknown past. It was around this time that the break-up happened. When she was in the thick of it, I asked her to look back to examples of times when she had faced difficult things before. She found this really hard, because she was so hurt, and the pain made it difficult to think clearly. But she stuck with the process and continued talking. As she did this, Simone started to find herself saying more positive words, then phrases and sentences, as we challenged and reframed some of the things she had been saying. Slowly, we were changing the narrative, the story she had been telling herself about the relationship, and about herself. She started to challenge some of the negative messages she had internalised, which she felt were no longer true. Simone found the inspiration within herself and allowed that voice to blossom, so she started to believe new, more positive things. Even though the journey was difficult, Simone could see just how much she had grown and got to know herself in the process.

We Can Do Hard Things and Sometimes it Takes Time

I often think that bereavement is like the ultimate break-up. Losing someone you love is one of the most devastating things most of us will ever go through, and yet it happens to people every day. We all know someone who has lost someone. It's something we fear deeply as humans. Sometimes my clients have asked me 'how long will I feel like this?' I say I don't know, but I think to myself, they will feel like this until they don't, and that there will be moments when the pain is not as great. That there will be times when they can be distracted for a short while before the pain comes back and that eventually there might be longer periods of time, that they may find that the quality of the pain changes and transforms into something else. And in between all of this, life goes on, time passes and wounds can heal. Sometimes the wounds are not ready to be healed. I have been asked to work with some clients who have been recently devastated by a loss. At that point, my job is to hold the space for them, to provide a safe place for them to talk and to listen. They are not ready for therapy at that time. The mind has a long journey of processing and catching up with what has happened before it's safe to do any therapeutic work.

I experienced a sort of delayed response to the passing of my dad, who I lost when I was nineteen. I don't think I really dealt with my feelings and grieved until some 10 years later. But when those gates opened, I was ready, and I felt it very deeply.

Decide to Choose Your Thoughts

I am a strong believer in the power of the mind, and I believe you can choose your thoughts*, to some extent. This means you can choose how you think about a situation, and that means you can change those thoughts and choose new, better ones. I am always amazed at how strong people are. I picked up 'How to Live When You Could be Dead' by Deborah James, (also known as Bowel Babe), already knowing what an incredible spirit this woman had. She wrote this book at the final stages of her bowel cancer journey, having co-presented a podcast called 'You, Me and the Big C' with Lauren Mahon and Rachael Bland, where the friends spoke about living with cancer. Deborah's book serves as a reminder to the people reading it, how incredibly short and precious life is. Although I cried at different points throughout the book, what really came through was her sense of humour and her determination to make the best of a terrible situation. It's a good reminder to have those examples when we might have a tendency to get stuck in our own misery.

One of my most inspiring clients was Jan, who I have learnt so much from. She needed help coming to terms with the neglect and abuse she suffered throughout her early life. Her boundaries were so violated in her childhood, that she struggled with asking for what she needed as an adult. Her parents were addicts and as a child, she was often left in charge of her younger siblings. One of her earliest memories was being left to look after a baby sibling, while she was under five herself. Jan described going to school hungry, and she spoke about her gratitude for the teacher who noticed her, giving her clean clothes to wear and books to take home. We worked together for an extensive amount of time to help her deal with her wounds around the pain she endured at that time. We talked about the people who let her down, her relationship with her parents, and how grateful she was to the people who helped her. Despite having such a difficult start in life and having to bear huge responsibilities at a young age, Jan grew up to have a happy personal life. She was able to form good relationships and have her own children, giving them the love and care she didn't have as a child. But she was still under the grip of her parents when she was an adult to some extent; she struggled with their demands for help to which she couldn't say no. When she embarked on therapy, she was sick of being under their grip. She wanted to get control over her life and to feel she could decide how closely to engage with them.

Using a variety of therapeutic tools, we worked on releasing her from the traumatic memories which were never far from the surface. Although Jan had been able to show her natural affection for her own son and daughter, she still needed to heal the little girl living inside her. We spent time healing her inner child, who appeared to Jan as a series of versions of herself: ranging from a babe in arms to an eighteen-year-old. Jan described the vivid images she could see of all of the incarnations of herself, lining up to greet her in her school hall. One by one, these versions of Jan came forward to be healed. This she did by listening to hypnosis recordings I made for her and imagining that she was spending time with all of her younger selves. She imagined herself playing records from her youth, brushing their hair, laughing and playing. After each session, we noticed that a few of the versions of her at similar ages morphed, so that there was one girl representing her at a certain age range. One day, Jan emailed me and said that there was only one girl left representing her younger self. In the session that week, we watched that eighteen-year-old walk out of the school hall and close the door behind her.

Jan put her heart and soul into her healing journey and eventually made peace with those traumatic memories from deep in her past. She emerged as a stronger version of herself and reconnected with her natural inner confidence, which she'd had as a small child. Jan was finally able to stand up to those who had bullied and mistreated her. Her unconscious mind was updated with more self-loving beliefs and her self-esteem was growing.

The Unconscious Mind Runs the Show

Most of what we do during the day are not things we have to think a lot about. It is estimated that more than 90% of the decisions and actions we take are run by the unconscious mind and we know that if we act as if something is already true, we can trick our minds into believing it is so. Imagine going to a work conference at a hotel. If I walk into a room where

I don't know anyone, thinking I am very nervous and I won't be able to speak to anyone, I will probably walk in, go and get a drink, and then sit down on my own. When I go to an event feeling open to the possibilities, I will find myself having conversations with anyone and everyone, feeling part of the event, because I have made some connections. I can use this natural way of being to help me in different situations. This is called 'acting as if'. You might say you feel nervous or shy about attending an event on your own, where you don't know anyone. You might say you would prefer to feel relaxed and confident about being able to say 'hello' to new people and starting a conversation. If you were to act 'as if' you were relaxed and confident, you would behave differently. Every step of your morning would be different, and every thought or word you say would be relaxed and confident and that would lead to feeling that way at the event, because you are acting as if you already have those attributes.

Even though it is a conscious decision to act as if you are already feeling the way you would like to feel, it's like a way to bypass the brain's thinking loop, which would usually keep you stuck in the same behaviour and pattern of thinking. Sometimes *behaving as if* we are more confident can lead to us being *perceived* as more confident, and that helps us to take more confident actions and so on, forming a virtuous circle of thought and behaviour.

The Sack of Beliefs

I often describe the unconscious beliefs we hold like this. Imagine that your grandparents each have a sack. Into their sack, they put all of their own beliefs, some from their parents, some from the society of the time, some of their own. They hand these sacks down to their children, who are your parents. Your parents bring their sacks of beliefs into their relationship. They examine some of the beliefs, throw some out, and add a few new ones of their own. As you grow up, you are exposed to these beliefs every day; they are an invisible thread that runs through everything you say, do, and think. At some point, you examine your sack and decide which beliefs you no longer want to hold on to. You form your own beliefs in this new time and space.

Then it is your turn to decide what to hold on to and what to let go of. You are growing, learning and changing in your own place and time, which is very different from that of your parents and grandparents.

EXERCISE 2A:

Examine your Beliefs

1. Download the template for Exercise 2 from:
    https://zeenatahmedpeto.com/book-bonuses/

2. Alternatively, use your journal or a piece of paper.

3. Write down any behaviours you want to change.

    E.g I am terrible at saying no to requests from X, I am not good at standing up for myself at work, I am always trying to please X and do what they want, I always go along with what the group wants rather than speaking up about what I want.

4. What is the belief that underpins that behaviour?

    E.g It is selfish to do what you want, it is kind to help other people, it is polite to let others go first.

5. Now trace back to find the source of the belief. What were you told or what did you see or hear that makes you believe that? Whose belief was that?

E.g. This comes from my mum. She always says it's important to be polite and be kind and put others first.

6.   Decide whether it is still a useful belief. Consider whether you can adapt it or decide to make a change and let this go now once and for all.

E.g. It is useful, but I have been following this all of the time, without thinking. It is healthier to adapt this belief or take steps to start letting it go.

The next three activities are separate but are related. You can download the templates at: https://zeenatahmedpeto.com/book-bonuses/

Alternatively, you can use your journal or pieces of paper to explore your answers.

EXERCISE 2B:

Your List of Achievements

1.   Think back over your life, looking for the positive moments. Consider those positives that you have had a part in creating as achievements.

2.   Now create a long list of everything you have achieved over your lifetime. Write down the age you were when you achieved those things next to each item.

You might include positive experiences starting with walking and talking, settling at school, any hobbies which you enjoyed, achievements in music or sport, friendships, connections with people who were important to you, activities you were part of, awards or certificates you gained at school, qualifications you earned, hobbies you enjoyed, skills you learnt, jobs you had, people you helped, new places you travelled to and so on. Continue the list into your adulthood with your education, career and relationships, travel, parenthood, and so on.

Some of my clients find this a helpful exercise as they find they remember things which they had forgotten about. It gives them a feeling of pride looking back over their younger self. Sometimes in that moment we may not have celebrated the achievement because we didn't realise how important that would be in the long run. You can do that now, looking back over the past.

When we are in a period of change, reflecting on what has gone before is a good way to take stock of our journey so far and encourages us to continue going forward.

EXERCISE 2C:

Your List of Challenges

1. Look back over your life and write down the challenges you have overcome, with the age you were when those events happened.

They might have been serious challenges, or they may have been periods of adjustment.

Here's an example of what you might include:

Birth, infant health, early childhood, home life, walking, talking, starting school, birth of siblings, illness in the family, bereavement, losing a pet, friendship challenges, moving home, break-up in the family, separation from family, illness in the family, disruption to education, moving location, starting a new school, personal health challenges, struggling with exams, starting work, going into higher education, finding a career path, relationships at work, personal relationships, etc.

2.   Write down the age you were next to the item in your list.

During those challenges, you had to adapt and adjust in order to cope with those situations. You may have had support from other people, be it family members, friends or professionals to help you, but you got through them. You also drew on your own resources and dug deep into yourself – often finding strengths that you may not have known were there.

When we face challenges, despite the discomfort and feelings of disorientation we might feel, we are given the opportunity to grow and to reach new heights. We are given the chance to rise to the challenge. Look back over your list of challenges or times you had to grow and adjust and acknowledge what you have managed to do. It is not often we congratulate ourselves for living through what has been a natural part of our lives!

EXERCISE 2D:

Journaling Exercise

Look at both of your lists. Write in your journal or on a piece of paper for 10-15 minutes, answering the following questions.

1. What did you have to put in to overcome those challenges or achieve those things?

2. What personal qualities helped you in times of challenge?

3. At which periods of your life did you have the most challenges or achievements?

4. Were they at the same or different times?

The caveat is that you can choose your thoughts with a healthy mind. If you feel you are unable to stabilise your mood or your thoughts, please seek medical advice and support from qualified professionals.

CHAPTER 3

You Need to Examine Your Life and Your Feelings

Examine Your Beginnings – Your Childhood and Before Your Birth

Think about your childhood. I want you to recall a few happy memories or one strong positive one from your childhood. And now bring to mind one or two strongly negative memories – from a time when you felt a strong *negative* emotion, such as fear or humiliation. If you compare the qualities of the two sorts of memories, you might find a contrast between how they appear to you. Positive memories tend to be more like a feeling, a *general sense* of a feeling of happiness and the memory itself might be hazy and indistinct, whereas the negative memories can often be in sharper focus, clearer and stronger. The reason for this is that it's the unconscious mind's way of protecting us. By remembering the negative memories more strongly, it can help us avoid such feelings as danger, pain, fear or humiliation, so the qualities might be sharper in terms of images or sounds. Happy memories tend to fade more quickly unless they are reinforced. Perhaps that's why we love taking photos to remember happy events. Looking at photos from our childhood can help us reinforce and create understanding around our memories by joining the dots between them with old photos.

Now think about what you know or have heard about your parents and their lives and circumstances. Where they grew up, and the culture and society in which they grew up would in time have a bearing on you, whether or not you were brought up by your parents.

I grew up in North London, the child of first-generation immigrant parents, who were born in pre-Partition India (later India and East Pakistan, now Bangladesh). My parents came to London in the 1960s bringing with them their beliefs and sensibilities from that place and time. The first time they were able to travel back to see their families was after I was born in 1973. The newly formed independent Bangladesh was recovering from war and my parents had been living in London for 10 years. I would love to know what they made of the place they stepped back into, after so much upheaval and change. As a child I didn't really know about the war, it wasn't spoken about at home, or maybe I just don't remember it. What I do remember was an emphasis on learning about my mother-tongue Bengali, and about my culture and religious identity. My parents were united in instilling in us their pride in their heritage and culture. There were inevitably gaps between my parents and me as I was growing up – some of their ideas seemed lost in translation. As a parent myself now, I am trying to keep many beautiful aspects of my heritage and culture alive with my own child, so he has a sense of that part of his rich cultural background.

The society and culture around you play an enormous part in who you are. Even though we were growing up in London, thousands of miles from our parents' countries of origin, the beliefs and values from those places loomed large in our childhoods. Let's return to Christos, whom we met earlier. His family, who hail from Cyprus, repeatedly instilled in him that he must always respect his elders and put others first. This was integral to being part of his family. These values have stayed with Christos throughout his life, sometimes to his detriment. One of the problems he faced was being too considerate of others, having a lack of boundaries, so he could not stand up for himself. Of course, being taken advantage of was not the intention behind the values his parents were trying to instil in him, but the messages felt unbalanced, so that they overpowered his own sense of what was right and wrong. Much of his therapy journey has been about finding out what *he thinks and believes for himself* and learning to have a stronger sense of personal identity. Through this, he has been able to politely fend off requests for his time and energy, which was a problem for him before. The underlying theme of putting others first, is still a part of his personal philosophy, but it has some caveats which help him to maintain his self-respect and he can now therefore gain the respect of others.

At the start of his therapy journey, he was being pulled in every direction by requests from his wife, siblings, and other family members, and he found it hard to say no to anyone. He felt it was so unfair that it was just *expected* that he would do these things and that he received very little thanks for his efforts. Christos was fed up with being taken for granted by members of his family and was hurt by the lack of consideration for him. During the process of changing his life, he decided not to maintain some of his relationships. He decided to keep those people at arm's length, with no direct contact on an everyday basis. Christos had been running away from this thought for years, because he felt so guilty every time he thought about it. Although he reduced his connection with some family members, he strongly maintained that he would always help them if they needed him, but at this stage in his life, it was not healthy for them to be as close as they had once been. This has been a huge area of healing for him, and he is much happier and stronger because of it.

For Christos, he learnt that fairness, honesty and kindness were amongst the most important values for him, and that's what he started to look for in his relationships. These were the values that were breached in his relationship with his wife, and when he looked back, that had been the case from the very start. Although he wanted to show his love for her in various ways, he felt that she didn't respect his ideas and that severed the connection between them. Due to his upbringing, he would let things go, avoiding conflict by keeping quiet. But deep down he felt hurt, and over time, the connection between them became weaker and weaker. Even though he was continually trying to please everyone around him, he ended up feeling rejected.

In our discussions, Christos decided that his values of fairness, honesty and kindness would help him maintain a strong relationship with his young child. He would create routines in their weekly diary, with activities for them to do together, including regular days out on Sundays. He would show his love by strengthening the bond and the connection between them. If Christos couldn't be part of his daughter's daily life, due to the breakdown of the marriage, he would work hard to maintain their father-daughter love and connection.

You Need to Be Honest with Yourself (No Hiding or Running Away)

It's time to take a long, hard look at your life, and be honest with yourself about your values. Which aspects jump out at you? You can find out what your values are by thinking about what is most important to you in life. What must feature in your life for you to be happy and what do you want to share with the significant people in your life? I wonder which aspects you love about yourself and your life and which ones you would love to change?

Most of the people I work with have some values in common. They are usually sensitive and kind, and they have compassion and empathy. A lot of men come to me for therapy, and I think they recognise these traits in themselves, which have not traditionally been celebrated as they are seen as more feminine traits. Many of them remark that they were told they were 'too sensitive' when they were children. These are the people I love working with, because when they have come to me, they are ready to gain more balance in their lives. They are also ready to embrace their natural selves. These values are wonderful, but like anything which is out of balance, there can be too much of a good thing. The clients I am describing in this book have often forgotten that they are also in need of kindness and empathy. By putting others first, they have inevitably put themselves last. They have often grown up with a pattern of trying to please other people, and this can be for different reasons. For some, it is a way of surviving with a demanding or difficult parent, in order to pacify them or keep them happy. Some of them wanted to gain the approval of their caregivers, or it could be that they were continually told that they should be stronger, bolder, and/or more confident. As a young child, my clients have internalised these messages to mean something enormous. If they don't live up to these ideals, they won't be loved; they are not good enough and will be rejected. These unconscious beliefs can rumble under the surface for many years until they are faced. It's now time to face those rumblings head-on.

Stop Pleasing Other People

Constantly worrying about what other people want, bending over backwards to put others first, or saying sorry for things, even when they are not your fault, can all be associated with people-pleasing behaviour. These behaviours stem from issues like low self-esteem or fear of rejection and trying to make the other person feel important can help people-pleasers to feel safe and part of the gang. As I mentioned earlier, these behaviours often stem back to childhood, where the young child understood that this was how to keep themselves in favour, which meant they were safe. Not all sensitive people are kind, and not all sensitive people have issues with their boundaries, but in my experience, often these traits appear together. These are the very people who find their way to me. As you work on your personal development, and start to improve your feelings about yourself, by valuing yourself more, your ability to think about your own needs grows. Not to the detriment of others, but in a more balanced way. Equally, having healthy self-esteem means you can have strong boundaries while maintaining your positive connection with others. Rather than trying to protect yourself from being rejected, you can engage in the relationship, confident that you will be met as an equal. The unconscious power struggle present in these relationships quietens and more balance and partnership can grow.

Doing What Your Heart Desires

Here's an example of how David (whom we met in Chapter 1), started to do more of what he really loved doing.

David absolutely loved spending time walking outdoors and was always keen to go hiking in his spare time. He would look through the shared family calendar with great longing, but seeing how disinterested his partner and children were, he would put it off for another time. After we started working together, I asked David to make a list of small things he could start to do, which would bring him some joy and happiness. Top of his list was walking. He found a social group of hikers online who had organised a hike and put it in his diary. David decided to hike with this group of unknown people, which was a huge step for him outside of his comfort zone. He reported back to me that even more than enjoying the walking, it was his sense of growth in himself that he loved. He treasured knowing that he had put himself first for a change and taken the time to do something he cherished. It was uncomfortable, and he would've loved for his family to come along, but it was better than missing out. He didn't like the idea of them coming along and not enjoying themselves, but I challenged him on this. I asked him to think about the countless times he had been to places he had not expected to enjoy but had ended up having a great time. Perhaps someone would have a lovely time because they were with him, doing something together. This exercise was much greater than the hike itself. It reminded David that he was a person with equally important needs and desires, and this was one small step towards doing things that he valued.

Face What You Are Trying to Ignore

Being honest with yourself includes facing what you might be trying to ignore. You have most likely come to the point where you are ready to take the next step and face these issues head-on. If you're reading this book, you might be seeking answers to help you prioritise what is most important to you. Once you decide to take the steps, it becomes easier to move forward with a sense of direction. As you develop, honour and deepen your own values, you start to recognise what epitomises you. These ideas become part of your map, and your values are the compass points, showing you the direction of travel. This becomes part of your legacy, or what you leave behind.

Get Comfortable with Your Resentments

We can hold on to resentments within our family of origin over decisions or comments our parents made, often decades ago. One client, Tom, said he was shy as a child, and this was compounded by the fact that his older brother was talkative and quite a show-off. Whenever they met with family or friends, their dad would introduce them as 'This is my eldest, and this is my quiet son.' Even though Tom would have psyched himself up on the journey, willing himself to be more confident and speak up, his efforts would be thwarted within seconds because of his father's comment. He later said that once he was labelled that way, his young mind felt he had to live up to that reputation, otherwise people would think his father wasn't trustworthy because he wasn't telling the truth! In later years, the absurdity of it all dawned on him. Something his father had said a handful of times in his childhood had stayed as a resentment with him into adulthood until he decided to confront it. As an adult, not speaking up was making it hard for him to seek promotions at work or discuss his needs in relationships. This comment, which became an unhelpful belief, had seeped into his unconscious mind and was having an impact on important parts of his life.

Listening to Your Younger Self

Similarly, there can be spoken or unspoken rivalries between siblings, which can go back a very long way. Often, they are about a perception of fairness and the idea that siblings were treated differently from each other. Sometimes this difference leads to the idea of favouritism. It feels unfair that one person is treated better than someone else, because they are the favourite. Children fundamentally believe in fairness and equality and find it hard to recognise that different people might have different needs, unless this is explained to them. Learning about the circumstances of why a parent might look as though they favour one child over the other can help, but resentments can still run deep. Sometimes a parent might find it easier to get along with a particular child due to their personality or shared interests, or they may worry about them more for some reason.

For Joanna, even though she knew her sister Emily needed additional support, she felt a bit resentful about all of the extra attention Emily got from their parents. Joanna felt responsible for looking after Emily whenever they were away from home. This meant Joanna couldn't just be free to play and enjoy herself, as she was always taking care of her sister, and was therefore missing out on something else. When we spoke about this, Joanna cited a few examples of times when she had to put her own desires to one side in order to stay with Emily, so she missed out on opportunities. Talking through the catalogue of times like this helped to ease her feelings of resentment. Often, these memories just want the chance to be spoken aloud, heard and acknowledged. By not speaking about them, we continue to give those thoughts potency and mystique. When they are spoken out loud, we can hear our younger selves talking about the experience we had at that time, *at that age.* As we hear them now as adults, we have a new perspective, more experience, and wisdom, and can see those thoughts in a new light. This helps us reconcile ourselves with those resentments from the past.

Gaining a new perspective with the distance and time from the events can help us to see the *positive intention** behind why someone said or did something. A parent may have looked like they favoured one child over another as that child had some sort of emotional or physical need which they were trying to fulfil. Having the perspective of time can help us understand the decisions our parents made for us and why.

Zoe told me that even some 40 years after she went to secondary school, she resented the choice of school that her parents had made for her. She was offered the chance to sit the exam for a sought-after grammar school, but her parents chose a local girl's comprehensive for her instead, thinking it was a better option for their child. They had a conservative outlook on life and had been brought up in a more traditional society in Greece, so they felt a single-sex girls' school was a better option for her.

Zoe had always resented this decision, as all of her friends went to the grammar school, which was more academic and seemed to have many more opportunities for their pupils. Looking back as an adult, Zoe felt deep down that perhaps they didn't think she could pass the exam. Perhaps they were trying to spare her the pain of rejection. This coupled with the fact that she wasn't asked what she thought, and the decision was made for her increased her feelings of resentment. She had felt that her education was adequate, but the atmosphere amongst her peers didn't encourage aiming high, and that was what she felt she had needed. Despite all of this, although she had different views, she later understood the *intentions* of her parents in line with their traditional views and values.

A Positive intention: There is an assumption in NLP (Neuro-Linguistic Programming) that 'behind every behaviour there is a positive intention'. This is to do with the motivation for the behaviour, not the way it is received. Even though the behaviour may not be deemed *positive* to the receiver of that behaviour, there is a *reason* why someone is behaving a certain way. It doesn't make their behaviour acceptable if you see it as negative, it just explains that they have a (usually unconscious) reason for their response (Steinhouse. R, Secondary Gain, Behind Every Behaviour is a Positive Intention, 2022).

Become Comfortable with Forgiveness

Forgiveness does not mean 'letting someone off the hook'. Sometimes my clients will tell me they are not ready to forgive someone as they don't want that person to get away with it, without some form of punishment or reparation. I believe that when we are ready to forgive someone, we are actually giving *ourselves the opportunity to heal*. Peter worked with me to heal from his experience of sexual abuse caused by someone in his extended family. Through this work, he was able to *forgive himself* first and foremost, as he had sadly carried the blame inside for many years. He felt guilty that he hadn't told someone, which could have prevented it from happening to someone else. Peter was also able to forgive other family members, who were completely unaware of what was going on. This experience was something Peter had not spoken much about, as it had become buried deep in his mind and only re-emerged after he became a father. The protective feelings he felt towards his child allowed the memories to surface after many years. He hadn't realised that he was still holding on to this anger until many years into adulthood, when he sought therapy and talked about the rage he felt about so much of his life. By working through these emotions, he was able to gain insights into the feelings of anger he was holding onto – towards himself and his parents, as well as the perpetrator. The anger which erupted when he was under stress, was taking over his life and he knew it was getting out of control. That was what brought him to seek therapy – this rage which was threatening to ruin his relationship. He had not once mentioned the historic abuse. Things improved over the sessions, but I felt there was something else which I couldn't put my finger on. At the close of his penultimate therapy session, Peter said there was something else which he wanted to talk about. That's when he broke down and let out all of the emotion which he had been holding on to. We arranged to continue with the sessions and that's when the real therapy was able to happen. The abuse had left him so afraid that he found it hard to trust anyone, with boundaries so robust that he repelled most people. When he met his partner, he was attracted to her open nature, and they hit it off straight away. However, his angry outbursts were becoming a problem. We worked on improving his self-esteem in the present and healing his younger self in the past. This helped him look to the future with hope and a more positive outlook for the future of him and his family.

Forgiveness is About Setting Yourself Free

By choosing to heal your feelings about the past, you are actively trying to reduce the potency of the pain and let the feelings go. You have agency. You are in control of the situation in the present because you can choose what to do with the knowledge you have. It's time to stop blaming yourself for the mistakes you have made and make peace with the positive intention* you had at that time. What were the reasons for your choices back then? If you think back and examine those, you can understand the motivation for your behaviour, even though you might not be happy with those choices now. Forgiveness is about setting yourself free. Perhaps the time is right to work on that now.

Forgiving Yourself for Your Mistakes is a Vital Step on Your Journey

Beth has forgiven her younger self for allowing other people to manipulate her in so many ways. As she looked back over her marriage, she realised that she gave away her power on the first day that she embarked on the relationship.

She has forgiven herself for trusting her former husband, and starting that relationship, when she knew it felt wrong. She allowed him to cross her boundaries and persuade her into saying yes, when deep down, she felt it was a no. Looking back, she had been used to her father disregarding her thoughts and feelings and replacing them with what he thought she should do. She later realised that he had been like this throughout her life, with her mother and sister too, so it was easy for Beth to allow someone else to step in and control her. Similarly, when she investigated her father's family history, this pattern of a controlling parent making all of the decisions was apparent in his family. He was repeating the patterns of a controlling parent and was largely unaware of the effects of his actions. She was able to forgive herself for her past mistakes and decided that this pattern would end with her.

Learning to Forgive Those Around You

Forgiving those around you is not about letting people off the hook. It's a vital phase in recovering from past trauma and taking the brave steps to move forward in your life. A lot of work that I do with clients is about reframing thoughts – Asking 'What else could this mean?' We challenge assumptions or outdated beliefs and update the database that the unconscious mind draws upon to make decisions. We work on the physical and emotional effects of the trauma, treading lightly to support safe recovery. An important part of trauma work is to ensure that the younger self, sometimes called the *inner child*, is helped to feel safe. Together we work on supporting that younger part of themselves to grow up free from those old emotions. Usually, the client concludes that what happened to them *is not about them*. It's often about the circumstances or other people who might have been older and wiser. As Dr Deepak Ravindran says, "Hypnotherapy has great potential in ...treating mental health issues around deep-seated trauma and its manifestation..." (Ravindran. D, The Pain-Free Mindset, 2021).

I shared the case of Jan in Chapter 2. She was the woman who faced neglect and trauma as a child and as a young woman. A great deal of Jan's healing was around forgiveness, as she wanted to understand what led to her parents' actions and choices. She suffered from chronic pain and illness for many years as an adult and was determined to heal from her past. Jan had limited knowledge of her parents' childhoods, but she spent time questioning relatives and visiting old family homes, to piece together the story of their lives. This was essential for her to be able to understand what led to her parent's problems, what drove their actions, and ultimately why they could not care for her. The pain of a neglected childhood has been a lifelong journey for Jan, which presented itself as widespread physical pain trapped in her body. For years, she had tried to put her past behind her, distancing herself from her parents. She finished school and started working, got married and had children. Jan worked hard to be the mother she herself had craved as a child. It was only when her own family had grown up and her parents were elderly and frail that she was able to start to take steps to healing herself.

Even though she had been running away from the past, her body remembered. These visceral memories were trapped in her body. Jan sought every type of medical intervention she could to release herself from the grip of the pain, which was debilitating, despite numerous types of medication and even operations. She was struggling to live and found that she couldn't enjoy anything anymore as her body was crying out, asking her to seek help. That was when it was recommended that she seek talking therapy and the floodgates opened.

In The Body Keeps the Score, Bessel van der Kolk says "Many traumatised individuals are too hypervigilant to enjoy the ordinary pleasures that life has to offer…" (van der Kolk, B. The Body Keeps the Score, 2014).

Jan examined how her early childhood trauma had led her unconscious mind to be so vigilant, always on red alert, leaving her exhausted from all of the effort that took. She started to understand that as a child she was naturally seeking the attention of her parents, which she did not receive, and this gave her clues as to why she had such poor boundaries in other relationships. As she had grown up, Jan had found herself constantly seeking approval and bending over backwards to please people, which left her vulnerable to being manipulated.

Through this work, she was able to see the connections and understand why she did what she did. Jan was able to reconcile with the past and forgive the adults around her for not being aware of her plight. She also chose to love her younger self, that frightened little girl who desperately needed love. Above all, she realised that this was *not about her*, and that her parents had suffered, too. They had made some poor choices but were coping the best they could. She was finally able to make peace with the past.

Over time, her body began to recognise that she was no longer under threat. All of the work she did helped her finally release her mind and body from the years of suffering. As Bessel van der Kolk says, "For real change to take place, the body needs to learn that the danger has passed and to live in the reality of the present." (van der Kolk, B. The Body Keeps the Score, 2014).

Jan continues to prioritise healing her younger self with loving thoughts and actions and is now enjoying a full life with her husband, children, and grandchildren.

If you are struggling with trauma, and are finding it hard to recover, seek help from a qualified professional.

Let Go of What is No Longer Serving You

There may be messages that we have internalised, which are no longer serving us. Maybe they are from another time or place and are no longer relevant today. Maybe we just don't agree with the message we received, or it's something about the way we have received and stored it inside. The good thing is, when we are examining our lives, we can choose to let go of what no longer serves us. It's time to let go of those beliefs or ideas that you suspect have been holding you back or hampering your progress. This is probably something very clear and obvious to you. For a number of my clients, this has come down to self-worth; how much they value themselves. They want to show more love for themselves, but they have been programmed to think about the needs of others first, and this has been a repeating pattern over their lifetime. Perhaps this resonates with you, or it may be a different thought pattern that you want to let go of. Allow yourself some time to conjure the memories of times when these beliefs were running the show. Now, we'll proceed with an exercise to help you release some of these thoughts.

EXERCISE 3A:
THOUGHT RELEASE AND LET GO

You can download the template from:
https://zeenatahmedpeto.com/book-bonuses/

You will need some plain paper, an ink pen, a bowl of water and a sink.

1. Take a sheet of paper and an ink pen.

2. Write down all of the examples of when that thinking pattern or belief was causing your behaviour. Identify that belief and label it. Choose one incident when the feelings were very strong. Think about that incident and pay attention to all of the details. Think about the consequences and how you felt afterwards.

3. Now write down as much detail as you can about the scenes you can remember and how you felt at the end of them.

4. Fill up both sides of the paper with your thoughts. Pour as much emotion as you can into them. Use another sheet of paper if you need to.

5. When you are finished, tell yourself you are going to discard those beliefs. You are letting go of them. They have served you for a reason, but you don't need them anymore.

6. When you are ready to let go of those beliefs, rip up the sheet of paper and put all of the pieces into the bowl of water.

7. Leave the bowl to sit for an hour.

8. When you see that the ink has been lifted from the page, pour the water into the sink. The ink should have lifted off the paper. Symbolically, it is as if the words have been erased and you are discarding them with the thoughts down the drain.

9. Say out loud 'I am releasing these thoughts.'

This is one step which can help you let go of these thoughts and patterns. The therapeutic nature of writing down your thoughts and symbolically washing them away can be a powerful tool when coupled with other actions. Each time you actively seek to let go of an old pattern; you are loosening its grip. It is also important to fill in the gap with a new, more positive and fruitful belief which will support your self-worth, for example. You may wish to repeat this exercise more than once, for example, once a week until the thoughts reduce and transform into more positive ones.

EXERCISE 3B:
SPENDING TIME WITH YOUR INNER CHILD

1. Find a photo of yourself as a child and connect with your younger self with your eyes closed.

2. Imagine a place where you felt comfortable as a child – in the park, in your bedroom, at a library. Meet your younger self there.

3. Build the relationship a little at a time, showing your love and care. Give your younger self time to become comfortable with you.

4. Tell your inner child that you are going to offer him or her what he or she needs the most. Give your undivided attention and unconditional love.

5. Provide him or her with what she needs now. You can hand over a book, a toy or something else that symbolises the love that you are giving to your younger self.

6. See him or her receive this gift and acknowledge your love.

7. Let him or her know that you are not far away, and that he or she can signal for you to connect when needed.

(Limmer. E, The Body Language of Illness, 1995)

CHAPTER 4

Talk to Your Partner About Your Feelings

It's time to be honest. To quote Shakespeare, In Act 1, scene 3 of Hamlet, Polonius says to his son Laertes 'This above all: to thine own self be true…'

Being Honest with Yourself

As you read this book, you will be thinking about your own life in the background. You will probably have most or all of the essentials in your life covered, but I wonder which areas in your life feel like they need more attention. What is missing from your life? And whether there is something you are craving that you don't already have? Does that missing part keep rearing its head and niggling at you?

Juliette has a successful clothing business which she has built up over 20 years with her husband. She has worked hard to create a brand and provide lots of opportunities for the staff who work for her and strive for success. But Juliette has ambitions for the next part of her life which include travel adventures and living abroad, perhaps living on a farm, growing her own fruit and vegetables and running a cafe. She desires a sense of freedom, living in a sunny idyll, but there is one problem. Her husband does not want to leave their hometown and all that they have built together. The longing she has is strong, yet she's torn between the two parts of her who want opposing things for the next stage of her life. Their marriage has been in trouble for a while and she is considering leaving him and starting again, but she's afraid to break this news. Juliette came to therapy to work through her feelings and figure out what she truly desires. She has started being honest with herself and that was her first step.

Be Honest with Your Partner

This can be the hardest part of the whole journey. Most of my clients are extremely sympathetic to their partner's needs and want to broach these subjects with sensitivity. Finding a time and place to be able to talk openly is crucial.

When we are thinking about our loved ones, we often want to spare their feelings, and we don't want to hurt them. I would suggest that it is critical to be open and honest in order to honour that part of yourself that wishes to be heard. I think that being able to speak from the heart is where true intimacy lies in a relationship. You are reading this book for a reason, and whatever your situation may be, there are things you might wish to do or that you dream about, but you find it hard to bring up. Perhaps you have tried and have seen that the response was not what you hoped for. Or you just know that your ideas won't be received well. It's important to discuss what you both need or want from the next phase of your life. Talk and listen equally and try to hear and read their message. What are they *not* saying that they might want you to know? Is their body language in agreement with their tone of voice and their choice of words? Only once you have laid your cards on the table can you consider how you can both have your needs met at the same time.

Open the Channels of Communication

It's important to set a time and space free from distractions for conversations to take place. Although this is beneficial for relationships at any time, it is even more important when you are discussing something that can make you both feel vulnerable.

This might mean creating a space free from time pressure, where you are not thinking about work, and any responsibilities like childcare are taken care of, allowing you both to be fully present and able to give each other your full attention. It can help to explain the topic that you want to talk about, so that they can be mentally prepared. Ensure that you choose a quiet and private space so that any emotions can be expressed freely. I find going for a walk and talking outdoors is a really good way of taking the pressure off. The movement of walking can help calm the nervous system and soothe the brain from becoming too overstimulated. Being outside in nature is calming as you are out in the natural elements, surrounded by harmonious colours and sounds. Walking together means you can be looking ahead and can glance over to see each other's responses. You can start the conversation when you have found a quiet spot to sit down. Being outdoors gives you the physical and mental space to be able to expand into it. It's limitless. When you are having a serious conversation at home with all of your personal belongings around you, it can make it more difficult. This way, you can return to the safety of home, leaving that conversation outside.

Come to the Conversation with a Kind and Honest Mindset

When you are thinking about opening up and sharing your feelings with your partner, you are probably thinking about how they will react. You are probably basing this on how they have been before, in your experience of interacting with each other. If you find yourself worrying about getting stuck into a certain pattern of behaviour, which hijacks the ability to talk openly, try a pattern interrupt. This is where you can change something small, which leads to a change in the pattern or the process of your conversations. The small change can have an impact on the way the conversation usually goes, because you have consciously created a diversion for the brain to navigate, and this means you can change the outcome. In this case, you are trying to help a conversation go smoothly and to avoid conflict.

In the case of Christos, he was aware of how vulnerable his wife felt every time they had a conversation about the state of their marriage. He had to persist with trying to communicate kindly and gently, even when she was disruptive and aggressive. He knew that it was her vulnerability that was causing her to behave this way, and over time, their communication improved. He interrupted the pattern of allowing things to escalate into an argument, by not engaging in that form of communication. This was changing a pattern which went back for years to the start of their 20-year relationship, so it took some time for this pattern to change. He persisted and kept reminding himself that this would change, if he changed the way he engaged with her.

Give Your Partner Time to Catch Up

Giving your partner time to catch up with new information is essential, too. Your thoughts may have been going around your head for a long time, but your partner may not know the reasons and nuances around your thoughts. Give them time to assimilate the new ideas and come back to the discussion when they are ready to ask questions. Be prepared to answer their questions, which may come all at once or sporadically, as they think of a new idea. Try to maintain an honest and kind mindset when you are faced with questions.

David noted that his wife often seemed uncomfortable as soon as he started to talk about making changes. She would start to become upset, and he found it hard to broach important topics. The way he helped her feel more at ease was to give her some time to get used to any new ideas. He brought up a topic and assessed her reaction. He asked if she was okay to talk about it now, or at another specified time. David would also text his wife from work in the morning, to set a time to talk about things. He also tried to keep the conversation punctuated in an enclosed space so that it didn't proliferate into every conversation.

Consider Mediation or Counselling to Help You Communicate

Sometimes outside help can be a useful way to help you forge a new way to communicate. Couples therapy with a relationship counsellor can take different forms, but a common way is to have an initial session together and then individual sessions with the same therapist. Sometimes both people attend all sessions together. These sessions can last from a few sessions to weekly sessions, continuing for a longer period of time. It depends on the style of therapy or counselling offered and what the couple is comfortable with in terms of time or budget. My own experience of having relationship therapy was eye-opening and helped change the course of my life. I learnt so much about myself and how I was relating to other people, both within the marriage and with other people in my personal and professional life. I became aware of my poor boundaries, and how being too kind was inadvertently hurting me. The therapy sessions helped me to navigate the process of breaking up and starting again in many senses and helped me to work out what I wanted instead of what I had. I continued to have sessions with the therapist after the break-up, to help me regain my sense of self and to help me get my confidence back. I wanted to be prepared to go it alone, and those sessions helped me do that.

Therapy can help you speak your feelings aloud to a professional. I know that for many people, they don't know what they mean until they *hear* what they say. Sometimes the words come out of the unconscious mind and reveal themselves before you even realise how you were feeling. Incidentally, I love the moments I get to witness when clients in my room reach a level of clarity or awareness. Some of them smile, some say, 'I understand!'. Some nod or start laughing. It's an incredible moment to see, and I often mirror their emotions and it gives me goosebumps. It is an honour to witness such a moment of clarity.

When you are speaking to a therapist, they are not only listening to you, but you are also listening to *yourself* articulate your thoughts for someone else to be able to understand. David says he benefits so much from talking in his therapy sessions, because he understands more about his situation as he speaks. As he explains his feelings and shares more information, it helps it slot into place and organises it in his mind as he is talking. He says the fog lifts by the end of the session, and he gains clarity about what he is going to do next, as he has discussed it. It is so much easier after talking, as his brain is familiar with what is happening, and he feels more comfortable going into a situation.

Consider the Different Phases of Your Relationship

When you are at a crossroads in the path of your relationship, it can be helpful to consider the following:

Remember How it Was at the Start

Many of my clients have said that there were signs from the start that this was not the best choice for them. In the case of Beth, strengthening her boundaries was one of the main areas of work for her. She said that when she looks back, she can see that she allowed herself to be persuaded into her relationship. She felt that this was not a good match for her, but she was not strong enough to say no. She realises now that this was the first step of walking into a relationship with her now ex-husband, where control would play such a large part.

Pinpoint the Moment or Time When it Changed

Zoe said she managed to pinpoint the moment when everything changed in her relationship. One evening, her husband sat her down and revealed his infidelity. Although she listened calmly and tried to understand his explanation, she felt like the world was ending. The marriage limped on; they showed their brave faces to the world and tried to carry on as before. They had both agreed they still wanted to be together. Yet, despite their best efforts, they could not save the marriage and they went their separate ways several years later. Looking back, she says it changed on that day because that's the day her trust was broken.

Consider the Positive Parts of Your Relationship

When you are unsure about the future of your relationship, the difficulties can stand out and swamp everything else. In the following exercise, I invite you to consider the positives which have come from your relationship or situation.

EXERCISE 4A:
THE POSITIVE MEMORY BANK

You can download the templates from:
https://zeenatahmedpeto.com/book-bonuses/

1. List all of the positive and significant events in your relationship which stand out in your memory. Here are some examples:

- Holidays

- Where you met

- Firsts

- Travel abroad

- Fun times with friends

- Parties, weddings, special events

- Early experiences

- Things that no one else knows about, because they weren't there

- Having children

- Happy milestone events

Incidentally, all of my clients who have children with their partner, have said this is the part they wouldn't change for the world. When you are communicating with your partner, it could be really positive to talk to them about some of these shared experiences and memories, regardless of the future of your relationship. It is possible to move forward feeling good about yourself, your relationship, and each other. Sharing positive memories and talking about the things only you two have experienced together can create a new positive regard and respect for each other.

Why This, Now?

When people embark on therapy, I often ask them this question. What has brought them to talking and exploring now? I ask them what is niggling at them or driving them to this change now? For most of my clients, these questions come up when they are at a crossroads in life. They are about to settle down with their partner, start a family, or their family has grown up and they are thinking about the next phase of their life. There is usually a transition coming up and that's when our unconscious minds can see a potential exit sign. This next exercise is about considering all of your options and trying out the different scenarios. Try this exercise when you have some privacy and can write freely for a length of time.

EXERCISE 4B:
REALITY AND DREAM LIFE SCENARIOS

You can download the templates from:
https://zeenatahmedpeto.com/book-bonuses/

1. Create two columns: A and B on a piece of paper.

2. Consider two (or more) possible scenarios for you in the next phase of your life. E.g. For Christos, he considered A: Living with his wife and child or B: Living separately and co-parenting. Juliette considered A: Continuing with her business and marriage or B: Moving abroad and starting a new life alone.

3. Write the titles of each scenario in columns A and B.

4. Now swiftly write down your instinctive reasons for each of those columns.

5. When you have finished, spend time reading over column A and imagining it in great detail.

6. Then read over column B imagining it in great detail.

7. Consider your gut response and write about it for 15 minutes without stopping to read over what you have written.

8. Go for a walk or take some exercise while you allow your thoughts to work themselves out.

9. Be open and allow any insights to emerge.

CHAPTER 5

You Are a Role Model for Your Children

Show Your Children How to Be Healthy and Happy

As we have seen from the clients' stories I have shared, what we say as much as what we do as parents has an enormous impact on how our children grow up. The mindset that we operate within and share through our thought processes, words, behaviour, values, and actions, contributes to the way our children develop and become adults. Their feelings about themselves and their self-esteem can be hugely influenced by what they have learnt in early childhood. If you have been living with and bringing up your children, you have been sharing your values with them from the moment they were born. Your values are related to what is really important to you in life, and usually, they underpin what you talk about, care about, and what you do. There is usually a congruence to them, so your values are a thread that runs through your thoughts, words, and actions. These are largely unconscious and are closely related to your beliefs, which are often passed down from your parents and the society you grew up in, as discussed in Chapter 2.

When you think about your values, they will have a natural hierarchy. What is most important to you overall? Being kind, working hard or trying your best, for example. Spend time working out the top values you want to *choose* to pass down to your children. You can create a motto or saying that you say to them regularly. A parent I worked with introduced the saying 'We look out for each other' into her home to encourage everyone to be considerate of each other's feelings and needs living in a home together.

Your Values are Revealed in What You Say

Your language communicates your values to your children, in the words you choose to use and the tone of voice and manner in which you speak. Christos, who wanted to be the best dad he could be, was concerned about his daughter growing up around raised voices and flippant remarks, which were common in her environment. Christos wanted to model a positive way of speaking, and he was scrupulous about speaking kindly and politely with his toddler, who, in turn, mirrored it back. By valuing kindness and respect as his top values, he was able to change the environment for his child, who started to speak to other members of her extended family in the same polite manner. This, in turn, changed the way they responded. Rather than despairing at the futility of the situation, Christos managed to create a chain reaction and a change in the way the whole extended family spoke to each other, just by changing *his* actions. As mentioned in Chapter 2, people will change in response to you changing, and you can create a virtuous circle.

Your Values are Revealed in How and What You Think

If you show flexibility and the ability to adapt, your children will pick up these ways of thinking. Approaching things calmly, with openness and the resilience to bounce back, will stand your children in good stead as they mature. It's important to call out bad behaviour or comment on things which you think are wrong. What you are demonstrating is that some things go against your moral code as a person and as a family. On a simple level, I always comment on my dislike of booing in football matches, which to me, feels oppressive and taunting.

Your Values Are Revealed in How You Behave

For Christos, one of his top values is to help others. He will always try to support someone who asks him for help and will go out of his way to help those in need. Part of that has been taking his nephews under his wing and being a constant presence in their lives after their father left the home. Despite finding themselves in a difficult and hostile environment, their uncle has shown them how hard work and kindness pay off. As he has worked so hard on improving his boundaries, he is also ensuring that he passes this on, too. He is a role model to these young people and they are absorbing and internalising his values by being around him.

Model How to Take Care of Yourself

Your children are absorbing information about how to live whenever they are around you, including how you look after yourself. Most of us give some thought to our health and being good role models for our children in terms of healthy eating and physical activity. Stephanie was finding that her teenage daughters were spending more and more time in their bedrooms or on their devices and that she and her husband would keep looking at their work laptops into the evening. They were inspired to make changes after they had a family holiday in Spain. Their friends had recently moved there and lived in an apartment block with a swimming pool and sports facilities attached. Stephanie's family discussed ways to make some changes to their family life. She decided to sign them up to their local health and fitness club back in the UK. The family would meet there on three days of the week, and they could swim or take classes together. The parents and children were all getting fitter and healthier, and they spent more time together because of these changes. Through their fitness regime, they were able to do fun runs and go cycling; activities which they were not able to do before. Stephanie showed her family that one of their family values was to take care of your physical and mental health. Showing their children how to prioritise their well-being was an important lesson for this family.

Taking Care of Your Emotional and Mental Health

Another area that we can no longer ignore is mental health. Fortunately, talking about our challenges is less of a taboo now, and as a society we have a greater understanding of the need to discuss how to keep ourselves healthy mentally. School curricula are already talking about strategies for overcoming mental hurdles and building resilience, and this is something we should also be discussing openly at home. As with anything, balance is important, so being open to talking about challenges should not mean *only* talking about challenges. Building resilience by reflecting on what has gone well each day is a positive strategy which focuses the mind on what you *can* do, rather than what you can't.

Sasha, a mother of two girls, reads extensively about positive thinking strategies and has been teaching her children daily practices, which they have woven into their family routines. They start their day talking about what they can expect from the day ahead on their way to school; anything they are looking forward to, and any potential challenges. They discuss what might help them to deal with those challenges. At bedtime, they talk about how things went and what they are grateful for, which leaves them full of love and gratitude. This builds positive feelings that they go to sleep pondering. My family and I often have reflective conversations around the dinner table, and at key times in the year—at New Year, on symbolic or important dates, after a holiday, and at the start or end of a school term. I find it's a warm bonding experience, reflecting on what we have experienced and achieved. It reminds us of the positive and all that we have to be grateful for.

Taking Care of Your Spiritual Health

Spiritual health is another area of our lives where we can guide our children and share our values. There are many ways to introduce a level of spirituality, which may or may not be connected to religion. For Noushin, religion provides a moral code, combined with a way of life, and regular practices and commitments. This is the way she and her family show their devotion to a higher power and how they connect with other people, through community and charity events. Her children have learnt her values through explicit teaching and from absorbing the way of being from their parents. For this family, the structure of religion helps shape their values in modern society and gives them compass points on an uncharted map. They enjoy both collective acts of worship and private prayer and they see their spirituality through that lens.

For many of my clients, the connection with spirituality comes in different ways. They might attune to this feeling when visiting places of worship, sacred sites, or places of historic significance. For me, visiting places which inspire wonder and awe often connects me to a feeling of spirituality. They could be historic buildings like the Hagia Sophia in Istanbul, monuments like Stonehenge or places of natural beauty like the Grand Canyon. Being outside in nature, in forests, or by the sea can evoke feelings of awe and a spiritual connection for many people. It's the feeling that there is something bigger than us, and we are only a tiny part of the cosmos, that can be extremely powerful. Listening to music, chanting, and prayer that connects deeply with your soul or watching someone create something extraordinary can be so moving and awe-inspiring. I have had profound feelings of connecting to my spirituality in so many places, especially when there is a sense of history to a place. To me, these are all ways of connecting with our spirituality and I try to ensure that I make time for experiences like these with my loved ones.

Remain Open-Minded

In Don Miguel Ruiz's book The Four Agreements: A Practical Guide to Personal Freedom, the third agreement is 'Don't make assumptions.' (Ruiz. M, The Four Agreements, 1997).

The four agreements are as follows:

1. Be impeccable with your words.

2. Don't take anything personally.

3. Don't make assumptions.

4. Always do your best.

Ruiz published The Fifth Agreement: A Practical Guide to Self-Mastery in 2009, adding

5. Be sceptical, but learn to listen.

If you find yourself jumping to conclusions, or making assumptions about something, ask yourself, 'What *else* could this mean?' This is a great way to reframe a thought before you start to believe it as a fact. Trying to see things from another perspective is not always easy for anyone, especially for children. You can ask them to imagine *stepping into the shoes* of the other person, and asking how they would feel if they were in that position.

Model Making Conscious Choices

Part of being a parent is showing your children that you are making conscious decisions about how you live your life. You can show them that you are not allowing life to just happen to you and that you are not a bystander, watching your life play out. You can be an engaged and decisive person, choosing your conscious thoughts and your next steps. Sometimes we must act 'as if'. This is a way of thinking which says, 'If I was the person who *could* (do the thing you want to be able to do), I would (do this).' It can be helpful to think of someone you know who has this ability that you would like. It could be a character from a book or a film, whose ability you can imagine borrowing, like a cloak. This sort of 'borrowing' of someone's mindset can help you act as if you have their ability to do that specific thing.

At a difficult time, Marianne learnt to 'act as if'. She struggled to get out of bed and live her everyday life while she was going through a difficult divorce. But she had two young sons, one of whom was very sensitive to her mother's needs and was quite aware if she was upset. Marianne came to therapy to help her to cope with the emotional challenges of separating from her husband while she came to terms with the feelings of sadness she felt so keenly. We worked on the idea of a persona. Who was *this person* who could cope with the feelings and manage everyday life? How would they present themselves in conversations? What would they know and believe about themselves? Marianne would step into that character every day – consciously choosing to cope in that moment, *as if she could do it.*

Over time, she didn't have to keep deciding and thinking about it, because she was becoming stronger, and she was more able to deal with the feelings that came up. By choosing to use the 'as if frame' each day, and taking one step at a time, she was able to help her children through what could have been a much more devastating time. Marianne used this way of thinking, while remaining true to her essence. She was not trying to be someone else, but was merely picking up a useful skill to help her through a tough time.

'Yet' is The Magic Word

Using the word 'yet' is a good way to instil the expectation and assumption that something will happen at a later time. We sometimes find ourselves saying 'Oh, I can't do that!' and one of the reframes you can use is adding the word 'yet'. If you are actively working on something and trying to make changes for the better, you can reframe that comment to 'I can't do that … yet.' This allows the brain to process the thought with the understanding that it will happen; it just hasn't happened as of this moment. This is the magic word for lots of children. As they grow up, they are expected to learn hundreds of new skills and pieces of information, most of which require practise to acquire a level of competency. When the inevitable frustrations come up, we usually remark about practising and taking our time, coming back to something after a break, and we point out the progress and the achievements. With my younger clients, I like to teach them about the magic of the word yet, because they understand that 'yet' means they will get better at what they are practising.

Your Values Show Up in Everything You Do

You are modelling your values to your children every day because of how you show up in the world.

How you choose to spend your time and energy informs your children on an unconscious level what you think is important in life. Tony Robbins says, "Where focus goes, energy flows. Remember, what we *feel* is a result of what we're choosing to focus on" (Robbins. Tony, Tony Robbins: Where Focus Goes, Energy Flows! [Social Media Post], 2023).

So if you are becoming embroiled in destructive or negative behaviours, arguments, jealousy, comparing yourself to others, and *not* taking care of yourself, this is what you are passing on, without meaning to. We all have choices to make every day, and this comes into sharper focus when we become parents. What we do matters because our children are absorbing attitudes and ideas, even when we think they are not watching.

I sadly lost my father when I was nineteen, but the lessons I learnt from being around him run through me into my life today. What I observed was that he left a positive impression on the people he met, because he was so warm and kind to them. He was a GP from the late 1960s until he passed away some 30 years ago, so he met hundreds of members of the public, and had a large extended family. He taught me that I might only have one chance to meet someone in my life, and that I should leave them with a good feeling about that meeting. I should leave a good impression. I have also absorbed the values of the importance of family from my parents, as I was lucky enough to grow up in a loving home where I felt safe and cared for. We always sat at the table for a home-cooked meal and talked and laughed together. I know there was much more that happened and there were the inevitable struggles and disagreements, but my overall impression is that we were safe and happy. I know I am extremely fortunate and that many people I speak to did not have experiences like that. However, despite our own upbringings, we can make the hard choices and changes we need to, so that we can create a happy and safe childhood for our children. One of those ways is showing our children what we think is most important in life.

How You React in The Tough Times

If it's tough being a parent when things are going well in a relationship, it's even harder when the relationship breaks down. I have supported clients around their childcare arrangements when they are separated and are working out how often each parent takes care of their child or children. This is often the most contentious and painful part of a split and needs to be handled sensitively. I often cite a couple as an example, who in my opinion have handled this really well.

When Molly and Stuart split up, Rory was under 2. They have brought him up together, but apart, discussing all of his milestones and his parents' evenings, his clubs and trips away. They have split their time according to their work needs and have both taken him on holiday at different times. Each parent has taken him to after-school activities, so they can both be involved in all parts of his life. Molly has been instrumental in maintaining their son's relationships with his father's family (her ex-in-laws), taking him to visit on birthdays and Christmases. Stuart has spent every Christmas morning with their son, at the family home where Molly and Rory still live. Although they both have new relationships, they have prioritised their son, who has grown up very secure as a result. Their new partners also had to embrace the friendly nature of their parenting, as they became step-parents. Bringing up their child has been a joint effort and as he approaches adulthood, I'm sure they would say that all of the difficult conversations and compromises have been worth it. I am sure Rory himself will look back one day and understand just how much importance both his parents placed on him feeling secure and happy.

I know this might sound like an idyllic example of parenting after a split, but I think the main takeaway is that they were always thinking of their child and the greater good. They placed him in the centre and all other decisions worked around what would be best for him. They had the foresight to see the bigger picture even when things were difficult, and they had to compromise and work together.

You Are on The Same Team

In this same vein, I think it's important to remember you are on the same team. Regardless of your relationship status with the other parent (or parents in a blended family), you have to remember why you are doing this! The easy option could be to get involved in tit-for-tat squabbling, but making hard choices and decisions for the benefit of the greater good of the family is the bigger priority.

Christos realised that the life he was living with Eleni was not making him happy. After all of their years together, he realised that they were growing apart. He was changing, and she was holding on to the impetuous ways of her youth, but now they were parents to a young daughter. Despite the many challenges that came his way, he always prioritised his child. He wanted the atmosphere around her to be one of love, where she was happy and secure in her relationships with her parents. Even though her parents could no longer be together, Christos wanted above all else for his daughter to feel loved and cherished, free to learn and grow into a happy child. Even though Eleni constantly put obstacles in his way and reneged on their agreements, he was the constant in his daughter's life that he had always promised to be. He saw the bigger picture and always tried to remember that, despite their disagreements, he and Eleni were on the same team. They both wanted the best for their child. Christos worked on improving the relationship so that he could create that reality.

Model How to Prioritise Happiness

One of the most important things you can model to your children is prioritising happiness. As I have said earlier, I believe we can choose to be happy*. Even amongst the most difficult circumstances, we can find the silver lining in any cloud, by reframing our thoughts and by actively *choosing* to be optimistic. We can choose to change our mood, and this makes our experience of life, for us and for those around us, so much happier. We all have a different set point, in that some of us are naturally more optimistic or happier at our base level, but with effort, the rest of us can work hard to change and improve that level. If you want something strongly enough, and you work hard at it, the chance of improvement is greater than if you do nothing at all!

The following exercise can help you change your thoughts and create a more positive outlook.

EXERCISE 5:
REFRAMING NEGATIVE THOUGHTS

Download the template from:
https://zeenatahmedpeto.com/book-bonuses/

Alternatively, split a page into two columns.

1. In the first column, make a list of any negative comments that you find yourself saying or thinking.

2. When you have completed your list, read the first comment. Now think of a way to reframe that thought, so that you can see the positive within it. What else could that thought have meant? What is a more positive way to phrase it?

3. Write that reframed thought into the second column.

4. Continue down the list, reframing each negative comment or thought.

You can show your children how to challenge negative thoughts or thoughts which bring down your mood. You will naturally model how you change habits for new, better ones. You may think that this is difficult, and you might be right. To start with, changing any habit is difficult. However, challenging thoughts to create new, more positive ones will start to lift your mood and change the way you feel about things.

Keep returning to this exercise whenever you feel swamped by negative thoughts and reframe them. In time you can start to reframe your thoughts as you begin to say them and catch them at the source.

If you find this difficult, think about a person you know who is a natural optimist. This is a person who expects things to go well, even when the situation might look bleak to everyone else. Ask yourself, what would *they say* if you told them this negative thought and how would they counteract it? Try to step into the shoes of this person and take on their way of thinking to help you challenge your negative thoughts. Incidentally, if you don't know any optimistic people, it might be a good idea to widen your net, so you can meet some. We are the company we keep after all.

I believe we can choose to be happy. The caveat is that a person with good mental health has more ability to choose. If you are struggling with your mental health, please seek medical advice.

CHAPTER 6

Honour Yourself and Your Happiness

Only you can change how you feel. It may sound obvious, but there is only so much anyone can do to help another person. Even with the best will in the world, you can try your hardest to help someone, but they have to *want* to make that change. The change can be as simple as this. It is deciding that from now on you are going to *choose to be happy.* It may not be easy, but if you can find the intention and then take the steps you need to take, you can make that happen. When I talk to a client for the first time, I am gauging how much they want to change. They might explain that they are sick of their problems, but I am listening for their *desire to improve.* I know that the more desperate they are to change their situation, the more likely it is that they will succeed. In therapy, the relationship between the therapist and the client is of utmost importance, but the best indicator of success is the client's amount of desire for change, and that has to come from within.

You Can Choose Happiness

This starts with making choices that serve you for your highest good. Looking back, you might be able to see some choices you have made that have not served you well. Consider why you made those choices; whether they were because you did what you thought was best at the time, or because you didn't think you had another choice? Your pledge from now on can be as simple as this. When you are making decisions, you can ask yourself, 'Is this for my highest good?' Sometimes the decision will be made for the good of others, because there may be times when you will want to prioritise the needs of others over your own. Most of the time, though, consider your choices to ensure they will be good for you. Gabby Bernstein, a prominent spiritual teacher, recommends we 'choose again' (Bernstein. G, Super Attractor, 2021). She advises that whenever we feel resistance or fear, we can first recognise the thought, and then forgive the thought. I also like to say thank you to our unconscious mind for flagging the thought up in the first place. Gabby then says to consciously choose a new thought; one which will create positive feelings and will help us take the next steps with confidence. She says, "When you practise the Choose Again Method, you'll slow down your mental momentum and begin shifting toward more positive and empowering thoughts. Bit by bit, thought by thought, you'll feel better and elevate your energy!" (Bernstein. G, Choose Again to Shift Away from Negative Thoughts, 2023).

You are reading this book because you want to make changes and you want to do what is best for you. You can choose your thoughts and choose what's best for you to improve how you think and feel.

Choosing Not to Live up to Your Expectations

In the case of Sophie (whom we first met in Chapter 2), she realised that she was living up to what was expected of her, but that did not make her happy. Sophie met her partner through a dating app and found herself in a whirlwind romance, which turned out to be a very toxic relationship. She had always been a sensitive person, who felt things deeply and was constantly told that she was 'too nice' as she was growing up. Her father was cold and disapproving and she spent a lot of time trying to make him proud of her. Moving to a new city for university was a challenge, but she made a group of good friends who were able to come to her aid when she most needed it. These friends were surprised at how quickly Sophie decided to get married to her new partner.

Sophie had learnt the responsibility of being a 'good wife' from her mother. She was expected to support her husband's business ventures and provide a comfortable home for him when he returned from work. Her husband encouraged her to leave her job, so that she could spend more time at home, and she was happy with this arrangement for a while, until she became aware of lots of dubious business transactions. At first, she could hardly believe the way her partner changed a few months into the marriage. Gone was the romance of the early days, and he became impatient and unkind. She had her suspicions about why he was being cold and deceptive, but she felt conflicted as to whether she was being paranoid and thinking the worst.

Sophie sought therapy to help her work out whether her husband was really deceiving her. The mixed messages, erratic, domineering behaviour, and constant deception was very confusing. Sophie didn't want to end the marriage so quickly, as she felt she would be judged by her friends and family. Yet she was afraid of his violent temper and started to realise he was trying to control her every move. She was taught to work hard, be supportive of her husband, be the 'good wife' and be discreet about his dealings. While in therapy, she began to notice the parallels between her situation, and that of her mother and father. When she asked them for help, they sided with her husband, and told her *she* was being unreasonable. It dawned on her that this pattern of a people-pleaser and a dominant character had been present in her birth family, and she replicated this as an adult.

I'm happy to report that as her therapy sessions went on, she gained a deeper understanding of why she had always accepted poor treatment from men. We worked on building her confidence and her boundaries. She practised what she would say and how she would behave in different scenarios, so that through mental rehearsal and listening to hypnosis recordings, she started to feel stronger each day. Fortunately, her university friends offered her a place to stay, and she eventually went to seek legal advice. On a practical level, we discussed how she could get back into work so she could become financially independent. As Sophie walked away from this relationship, she had regained her independence and had a new-found self-respect. She decided to leave the expectations behind and honour herself and her happiness.

Having Healthy Boundaries

Being a kind, sensitive person is a beautiful thing. This probably means you are thoughtful of the needs of others, but it could also mean that you have poor boundaries. A boundary is an edge which marks the limits of an area, but in holistic terms, it means the part that says 'this is me, this is mine' and outside of my boundary is 'not me'. For many kind, sensitive people, this is a problem area because they often let people into their hearts too easily. Their boundaries are not robust enough to keep other people out. They might trust easily and have empathy for others. They can also have a deep desire to be *liked* and to be accepted as part of the gang. This can make it difficult for them to say no to requests. Some of this comes down to nature, and some to nurture, but in my experience, the two have to go hand in hand to create this situation. If you have the temperament and traits of someone who wants to put others first, you are more likely to encounter people who are happy to take from you. When you have traits like these, you can be more susceptible to attracting people who want to get their way. They can end up taking advantage of your considerate nature and pushing your boundaries. Those people have a need to be dominant, so unconsciously they are looking for someone they can push around. For people with weak boundaries, these behaviours are familiar. You have most likely encountered this before in your early life, in your family of origin. You could have seen it around you, or you could have experienced it yourself or between family members. That's why your unconscious mind *knows exactly what to do* to placate the other person and allow them to have what they need to be happy.

Some of my clients say they used to find it hard to hold their own position in a discussion, or form their own opinion, because they were not able to do this when they were growing up. Perhaps they were not listened to, were teased, ignored or ridiculed. For many people, experiences of bullying can happen several times over the course of their life, starting in the playground and carrying on into later life. When domineering characters push their weight around and put down people they see as weaker, they are often revealing their own weakness: a fear of being pushed around themselves. In many cases, their boundaries have also been breached, which, in turn, causes them to bully other people.

Taking on Too Much

One of the symptoms of having weak boundaries is that you can be more likely to take on a lot of responsibilities. There is a saying 'Ask a busy person if you want something done', because those people are often efficient with their time and can manage multiple projects at once. It may be that those people are good at delegating, and bringing in help and support to carry out what needs to be done. It's when we feel the need to do everything *ourselves* or that we can't say no to a request that it becomes a problem. This is when we can take on more than we can manage, which can lead to us feeling overwhelmed. People respond differently to requests, depending on several things. Some people are good at defending their boundaries in terms of their time and energy. They are able to easily say no; they cannot take on a new project because they are already committed to something else, or they simply don't want to. They can express this firmly and politely. This can be hard if you are sensitive to the needs of others, because your focus is on them, not you. Our beliefs and values come into play again here. There is a feeling that people 'should' or 'ought to' do something, and this comes from beliefs instilled way back, probably from their childhood.

David (whom we first met in Chapter 1) was such a person who always took on too much. He felt a huge responsibility to keep working very hard in his corporate job, whilst single-handedly running the home. His wife often needed his support, his young adult children were busy with their studies. At work, David was given more and more responsibility and the workload was growing. In an ideal world, David dreamt of living abroad and starting his own venture. He also knew in his heart that this dream would have to wait because he had so many people to think about. Despite the effort he put into all areas of his life, David felt he couldn't make any changes because everyone depended on him. He felt it was *his job* to be the strong one and keep going for everyone else.

In therapy, he considered all of the different ways he could ease his burden. We worked on strengthening his boundaries so he could stem the tide of more work coming to him, and he started to delegate and trust his team with more tasks. In time, David employed someone to do some chores once a week, which relieved some pressure, and he spoke to his adult children about helping out more. He realised that taking on too much was dragging him down, and that only he could change that. Not everything he was doing was necessary; some of it was a 'nice to have'. This process helped him examine and streamline his life, which gave him some of his precious time back.

Clear Expectations Help You Protect Your Boundaries

Omar was a very kind boss, which was admirable, but he was kind *to a fault*. He would turn a blind eye when most people would have sacked their employees for their conduct. Even when his employees broke rules and made major mistakes, Omar would consider their personal situation with great empathy, and respond leniently in a bid to protect them. Although he knew this was not the best solution, he had a deep need to be liked and therefore couldn't bring himself to reprimand his workers.

Consequently, the books were often not balanced, and he knew he had to make some personal changes. Since he has admitted all of this to himself, he has worked on creating stronger boundaries between himself and his employees. Omar no longer responds to messages in the evening, to protect his personal time. He has drawn up a code of conduct which he conveys clearly in staff meetings. Omar has asked some of the staff to leave and has started afresh with the new team. He now feels they respect him more than before because he is now working with integrity and does what he says he will do. This is better for him, and the clarity around the boundaries and expectations is better for his employees, too. The business is in better shape than it has been in for years and the burden Omar used to feel with dealing with his staff has gone, because everyone knows what to expect and they can all play by the very clear rules.

Strengthen Your Boundaries to Honour Your Happiness

One of the ways to honour your happiness is to improve your boundaries. Until that happens, other people can still take you for granted, take advantage of your kindness, or treat you like a doormat. One of the ways you can consider your boundary is 'this is me' and 'this is not me'.

Think about your skin, which is the biggest organ in the body. It is a living, breathing thing which is waterproof, but it's breathable and strong. It is the barrier between us and the outside world, and it protects our body from chemicals and bacteria. Skin can be repaired by the immune system if it is damaged and is also sensitive to its environment. It can sense changes in temperature and can protect us from the elements. It is the natural boundary between us and other people, us and the outside world.

In the same way, we have boundaries that we cannot see, but that act as a buffer for our emotions. This buffer helps us to filter what we let in and out, and it allows us time to process the information that comes in. We might know people who are able to protect their time and energy and only say yes to things that they are happy to do. This does not mean that they only do what they want; it means when they agree to something, they do it with a good heart. They don't feel compelled to do things or feel under pressure because their boundary is good at filtering out what may not be good for them. Of course, there *are* people who do tend to become selfish, only thinking of what serves them, but not others. There is a happy balance somewhere in between. Healthy boundaries are related to high self-worth and self-esteem, and as you prioritise valuing yourself, your boundaries will become stronger.

I'm here to tell you that you absolutely *can* improve your boundaries and still be a kind and caring person! This is not an either-or situation. In fact, you will mostly find that people around you respect you more when you are firm about what you do or don't want to do. When you first decide to make changes like this, they may come as a surprise to those around you, but after the initial surprise, which will take some adjusting to, this will become the new set point. I think it makes any transition easier if it is introduced gradually. Once people have had a little time to adjust, you can introduce the next micro change. By bringing these ideas to your attention, I think it's possible for all of us to make the changes we need to be able to create more balance in our characters, whilst honouring who we naturally are.

EXERCISE 6A:
RECOGNISE AND STRENGTHEN YOUR BOUNDARIES

Download the template from:
https://zeenatahmedpeto.com/book-bonuses/

Alternatively, take a sheet of paper or your journal and answer the following questions. Listen to the first answer that comes up and write it down.

1. If you could see your boundary, what would it look like? Describe the following:

    *   Colour =

    *   Shape =

    *   Texture =

    *   Size =

    *   Temperature =

    *   Thickness =

    *   Any other attributes =

2. If your boundary could speak, what would it say?

3. Does your boundary look like or remind you of anything?

4. Can you perceive any gaps or areas of weakness?

5. Spend 5 minutes each day strengthening and improving the health of your boundary. Listen to gentle meditative music and

imagine that you are repairing and strengthening the boundary. You can imagine helpful qualities like self-regeneration, flexibility, or self-compassion to help you strengthen your boundaries.

Read through the following exercise one step at a time. Give yourself time to be able to imagine in between the instructions. NB: It may be easier to close your eyes for the imagining part.

EXERCISE 6B: 'TRY ON' HAVING STRONG BOUNDARIES

Download the templates from:
https://zeenatahmedpeto.com/book-bonuses/

Alternatively, write on a sheet of paper or in your journal.

1. Think about someone who you look up to or admire *who has strong boundaries*. This could be a friend or acquaintance, or it could be a character from a book or a film. This could be a person who has values like yours, or they could be very different from you. Notice their strong sense of what they need to be comfortable in themselves. They can help you become a better version of yourself by helping you strengthen your boundaries. Spend a few minutes imagining this person.

2. Now write down a list of the key attributes of this person who you admire. What are the qualities that help them have healthy boundaries that you would love to adopt?

3. Name a situation where you find it hard to say no. Write down the qualities or strengths this person has, which you could employ to help you.

4. 'Try on' the quality in your mind *as you imagine yourself* in the situation with the ability to say no or do what is right for you. It might help to close your eyes as you imagine it.

5. Ask yourself 'What would X do here?'. Imagine what would happen if you were able to take on the attribute you admire. How would things be better?

6. Spend 5-10 minutes writing about what you discovered, using the questions above as prompts.

EXERCISE 6C:
'STEP INTO' HAVING STRONG BOUNDARIES

Download the templates from:
https://zeenatahmedpeto.com/book-bonuses/

Alternatively, write on a piece of paper or in your journal.

Exercise 6c takes this idea a step further. If you are happy with the person you chose for exercise 6a, you can continue with them, or you can choose a new person.

1. Choose a person or character whom you admire who has strong boundaries. This person has a quality or way of thinking you would like to be able to emulate. You do not have to like everything about them! They may have flaws, like all humans, but they have one crucial part that you would like to learn from.

2. (Close your eyes for this part if it helps)

   Imagine that you are looking at an enormous picture which is projected out in front of you. You are watching the person you admire in a situation that you might find difficult, but they are able to manage well.

3. Watch them very closely, noticing how they move or what they might say. You are watching them excel at communicating clearly and being able to maintain their boundaries with another person or people. Allow yourself to pick up any clues and information about how they are thinking when they are doing these activities. Step into their mindset of what makes them believe those things. When you have a strong sense of knowing, you can open your eyes.

4. Write down anything you remember from what you observed or felt.

5. (Close your eyes again for this part)

   This time, imagine you are walking over to the enormous picture, and you are going to *step into the frame*. Walk into the body of the person you admire, and as you do so, take on the attributes of having strong boundaries. You are now able to do what they did, in the ways that they did them. See yourself communicating your needs clearly, expressing what you would like to do. Notice how you are able to create a healthy boundary with your words and actions, whilst remaining calm and pleasant. Notice how the other person or people are able to accept what you say.

6. When you have finished imagining, open your eyes and write down anything you remember or learnt from your experience.

CHAPTER 7

You Have More Capabilities Than You Know

The Human Spirit is Very Strong

You have been through a lot and have survived life so far. You are more resilient than you realise.

You may know other people who have been through a lot over their lifetime. When you think about the events of a friend's life, you can see the achievements they made and the challenges they faced, even if you only know the main events. There is so much we can learn about the human spirit and people's capacity to manage and cope with adversity.

In Andrea's case, her early years were challenging in a number of ways. Being a gentle and thoughtful child, she found the world a confrontational place; where she felt bombarded by new things and remembers being described as 'too sensitive' by some of the adults around her. She didn't enjoy her friends' birthday parties – they were too loud and raucous and she much preferred to socialise with one friend. She often found the playground a bewildering place and stuck closely to the teachers on playground duty. Andrea's parents were learning how to cope with the challenges of bringing up a sensitive child and did what they could to support her. She could spend hours reading and escaping into her imagination, playing detailed games with her dolls and teddies. Her childhood was full of the usual challenges, but she faced her biggest shock when she lost her mother at 16. Andrea struggled to cope with the all-encompassing feelings of grief and the pressure of school life. She enjoyed focussing on her studies but found herself becoming isolated as her friends didn't know how to relate to her anymore. Andrea was depressed and they did not know how to help her.

She had lost interest in life whilst grieving the loss of her mum. This was the point at which we met, and I supported her to see her gifts and strengths through the grief she was struggling with at the time.

Once at university, Andrea started to express herself more freely, as we continued to work on finding her voice and discovering what made her heart sing. She found a group of like-minded people who loved Literature, music and the arts as much as she did. She joined societies where she found she could indulge her interests and took on some leadership roles supporting new students. Her gift of empathy became useful as she supported students who were struggling to fit in.

Now in her adulthood, Andrea can see how her challenges helped her to grow into who she is now. She has understood her challenges and saw the growth that came out of them, and knowing her personal strengths has helped her create more success in her life and career. Andrea has a great understanding of young people and volunteers at a local school listening to children read on her lunch break. She has formed good relationships with a few sensitive children whom she has supported over the past couple of years. Despite the difficulties, looking back, Andrea can see just how much growth took place after the sad passing of her mum. She has worked hard to make the best of that difficult situation.

Doing the Inner Work

Bobbie was having problems in lots of areas in her life and was becoming sick of the job she'd had for years. In a decisive moment, she moved out of the city and into a rural village. The sense of peace she felt was immediate, and the novelty of her new life was very exciting. However, within a few months, it dawned on her that the problems she thought she had left behind were still apparent. Deciding to uproot and move to a new place was a knee-jerk response to feeling stuck for years. She had made a big bold gesture, thinking this would solve the problem, but the unresolved issues inevitably crept up again. Much later, after numerous struggles, she came to realise that she had to do the *inner work* on herself to allow the peaceful life she so desired to begin in earnest.

What Are Your Superpowers?

When you are looking to make changes and to upgrade your everyday experience of life, you might start from the outside. Looking at the places you spend time – at your workplace, your home and the places you frequent. You might look at your relationships, who you are spending time with, who you want to connect with more or move away from. But a huge part of this work is about looking at yourself, and how what you put into life is reflected back at you. This work is an inside job. It's not *just* about letting go of things outside of yourself that no longer serve you. This work is about taking a 360-degree deep dive into your superpowers and what makes you tick.

How to Find Your Strengths and Weaknesses

Are you aware of your strengths and weaknesses? I find that many of my clients find it hard to pinpoint these without outside help, so I direct them to try indicator tests, which can give some useful extra insights. The main ones I use are 16 Personalities, which is based on the Myers Briggs Type Indicator (MBTI) and is created by NERIS Analytics (www.16personalities.com) and VIA Strengths Finder (www.viacharacter. org) created by the VIA Institute on Character, based in Ohio, USA.*

I find these tests useful, as they give a comprehensive assessment based on how you respond to numerous questions. We often think of our strengths as something we were praised for by others – which may or may not be accurate or may be out of date. These assessments are available online, in 30 languages free of charge and have been taken nearly 100 million times as cited on the 16 Personalities website (www.16personalities.com/ our-theory).

Get to Know Your Weaknesses

The same goes for our perceived weaknesses. We may have been criticised by our parents, friends, or partner and it can be difficult to see past the sting of criticism long enough to see the gift behind it. You can consider your key natural strengths as those things which help you to achieve your goals. When you have an idea for something, what happens? Maybe you are creative and can come up with ideas or solutions. Or perhaps you are determined to see things through to the end, or maybe you take your responsibilities seriously and want to do your best. All of those strengths sound great, but I want you to also look at their shadow side. When you are determined and are working hard on your creative idea, because you are responsible and want to do an amazing job, you might do it to the detriment of something else. This is where a weakness might appear, as something that can hinder your progress or well-being. Maybe you have a harsh inner critic whose voice holds you back from trying something, or you may have thoughts telling you that you are not capable of starting things or completing them. My advice is to get to know these areas of weakness and give them a label. Things are much easier to deal with when we have a name for them.

*This is correct at the time of writing, but you can do your research and find current tests *that are available and are used in the professional sphere.*

Your Character Strengths

The 24 Character Strengths, categorised by Virtue (viacharacter.org, no date)

Wisdom	Creativity	Curiosity	Judgement	Love of Learning	Perspective
Courage	Bravery	Perseverance	Honesty	Zest	
Humanity	Love	Kindness	Social Intelligence		
Justice	Teamwork	Fairness	Leadership		
Temperance	Foregivness	Humility	Prudence	Self-Regulation	
Transcendance	Appreciation of Beauty and Excellence	Gratitude	Hope	Humour	Spirituality

This table shows the 24 character strengths, categorised by six broad virtue categories as set out by the Via Institute on Character. As Martin Seligman explains, "…we see these six virtues as core characteristics endorsed by almost all religions and philosophical traditions, and taken together they capture the notion of good character." (Seligman. M, Authentic Happiness, 2003)

On the Via Institute on Character website, members of the public can take a test for free and receive their unique character strengths profile. Once you have taken the online questionnaire, you will be sent your character strengths report, listing your results in order from highest to lowest. (www.via.character.org)

Play to Your Strengths

What do you consider to be your natural strengths? These are the personality traits or ways of thinking and being that come naturally to you. You find it hard *not* to do them. It is logical to make the most of your natural gifts and talents because they make an impact with the least effort, and you will know what they are because they will feel right. Try out the tests mentioned here or similar ones to help you find and name your top strengths. Pledge to work on yourself with small daily habits which can help you to harness the power of your natural gifts. Work out the areas where you want to invest time and energy.

Consider your life purpose. What are you aiming towards at this point in your life? Notice the habits, the ways of speaking, thinking or behaving that you want to let go of and the strengths you want to shine a light on. How will you use your strengths to help you steer towards your life purpose? Consider working with a therapist who can support you if you need it.

The Unconscious Mind is Always Trying to Keep You Safe

Have you ever wondered why we remember frightening events and memories in so much detail?

It is because the unconscious mind holds on to every piece of information that it thinks could be useful, so it can prevent the scary thing from happening again. The details are stored in order to ensure that you can be alerted if there is a match. That's why it uses all of the senses to hold on to a memory.

When we have a memory of a happy time, like a day at the beach or the funfair, the memories are usually hazier and more incomplete. There might be a general feeling of happiness attached to the memory, with a few details that stand out, rather than a blow-by-blow account of the event.

I have a happy memory of a visit to the Isle of Wight with my parents, when I was a teenager. I can only remember snapshots of the trip, but one memory which stands out was the three of us sheltering from the rain on the beach and trying to pack up our picnic. Even though our afternoon had a soggy end, we were laughing so hard, chasing after bits of our picnic, being blown along the beach. I am left with a general sense of happiness, togetherness, and love. This example shows how hazy a good memory can be, compared to say, a memory of a serious argument. The unconscious mind would have been very vigilant and stimulated when the argument happened, and it would've taken lots of snapshots to ensure that you would be aware next time before it happened again. The unconscious is always listening and it's always awake, even when we are asleep.

Engaging the Unconscious Mind to Create Change

You can use the unconscious mind to help strengthen your natural capabilities and use them more in your everyday life. This is how I help my clients with hypnotherapy. The relationship between the conscious and unconscious minds can be imagined as a large, slow elephant with an agile monkey on its back. The elephant moves slowly, remembering everything, while the monkey flits from one idea to another. People who are highly attuned in their minds show "…a high quality of the relationship between the conscious and the unconscious." They also know that this relationship is "…an ongoing process, an evolution which is continually enhanced as time goes by." (Dilts. R, From Coach to Awakener, 2003)

Building on Your Strengths

The more you use a strength or a capability, the stronger it will become, just like a muscle. When I took the VIA Character Strength test many years ago, I was embarrassed to note that 'Bravery' was the last strength on the list. I decided to make a list of things which seemed scary to me, which would require me to be braver. I set myself a challenge to do more things out of my comfort zone and worked on those for a year. The following year

I repeated the test and I was happy to see that 'Bravery' had jumped up the list to number 16. I had improved my *least strongest* strength, by practising it.

The Power of Visualisation

You can find a lot of inspiration outside and bring that into your life, too. You may know others who have been through similar situations and have emerged positively out of the other end of it. Or there may be characters in books or films who you identify with and feel inspired by. The power of visualisation is immense, so what we expose our minds to, in terms of imagery, words, conversations and the energy around us can have profound effects, both positive and negative. If you are exposed to negativity, you will eventually become more negative in your thinking, unless you take yourself away and redress the balance. Surrounding yourself with the idea of possibilities is so much more inspiring and rewarding.

When I left my first full-time teaching job, I was nervous at the prospect of having to make a leaving speech. I knew I was going to feel very emotional. I had been at that job for 10 years, through my 20s and into my 30s. My time there was peppered with lots of pivotal moments in my life, and I had made really good friends there. I created a visual presentation full of photos to sum up my thoughts and feelings and invited my colleagues to watch it. What I hadn't realised at the time, was that I had created a vision board. The last screen showed pictures of all of the exciting things I was planning to do when I left, including travelling around the world, a new job, a new home, and a new relationship. On this one screen, I had assembled a collage of photos of what I was planning and hoping to achieve, experience and learn. They all seemed thrilling and daunting at the same time. Some had a longer time frame than others, and some had question marks around them. But within two years I had achieved all of those things. By simply putting my ideas out there into the world, I had given them life, and a space to breathe and grow. I gave myself the chance to imagine that I could change my life. Many of my clients really benefit from finding words or images that sum up what they are working towards.

They often use them as a screensaver, or print them out and stick them up somewhere, so that they are seeing those images regularly, which keeps the dream at the forefront of the mind, but still under the level of conscious awareness.

See Bonus Exercises for instructions on how to create your own vision board.

The Power of Visualisation Combined with Your Strengths

Visualisation is a powerful tool, which most of us use regularly. Some people are very good at imagining what is going to go *wrong* in their future. They worry that they might be late leaving home in the morning, so they will miss the train, end up late for work and will be playing catch-up when they have to give a presentation to their boss at work. They might then feel bad about themselves and end up having to work late to make up for the time they were not as productive as usual. When I meet some of my clients for the first time, they often don't realise that they have been using visualisation for a long time – to imagine the *worst*. They are often thinking of the worst-case scenario. But given what we know about the power of the mind, we know that we can learn how to visualise positively. By doing this, we can teach our brains which positive things to expect and how to be flexible in creating them.

Can Visualisation Alone Improve Performance?

In an experiment conducted at the University of Chicago, three groups of basketball players of similar age and ability were given a task to complete. The idea was to see whether visualisation could support their performance in shooting balls into the net. Their performance was measured at the start. Then, Group A were asked to practise shooting the ball into the net for one hour a day. Group B were asked to *visualise* shooting the ball into the net for one hour a day. Group C were asked to do nothing, no practising, and no visualising. All of the other conditions for the test were the same.

After 30 days, all of the groups were tested to see which group's ball shooting performance had improved the most. Which do you think it was? If you are like most people who read about this test, they would say – Group A, because they practised in real life. If you said Group A, you would be right. The results showed that group A *had* made the biggest improvement – of 24%. Interestingly, Group B had improved by 23% (*only 1% less* than the group who practised in real life)! As expected, Group C made no improvement.

So how does this work? How did Group B, who only visualised, make so much improvement, and only 1% less than the group who actually practised? By visualising a series of connected body movements, noticing where they were placing their attention, focussing on the pattern of their breathing, what was going through their mind, they were mentally rehearsing repeatedly in detail how to throw the perfect shot. When they were visualising, they shot the hoop perfectly and *never missed*. So, when they were tested after 30 days, their brains were primed for success and knew exactly how to shoot the ball into the net! The Group A players sometimes missed when they were practising, but the visualisers of Group B did not. We know that the mind can experience the visualisation as if it is real, and that makes it easier for us to create the performance or experience that we would like. (www.breakthroughbasketball.com, no date)

As you can see from this example, the scope for improving performance in sport is huge, and professional teams often have a raft of sports psychologists supporting them to reach their goals. Mindset and visualisation work is huge in sports performance, and you can use these ideas to support you in everyday life.

The best way to make visualisation work is to use all of your senses, especially your sight, sense of sound, your sense of touch and the emotion attached to it. It is also important to not only *see yourself* doing the thing you want to create, but also imagining that you are looking through your eyes *in the first person* and are embodying the position of the doer. In the example of shooting a ball through a hoop, you could imagine the feeling of the ball in your hands and feel your feet in position, watching your hands push the ball up, lining up for the perfect throw. You could hear the sound of your shoes on the basketball court, and as you watch the arc of the ball, hear the ball bouncing into the net. You will be breaking up all of the micro-steps which make up the perfect throw and this instructs your brain on exactly what to expect in real life. By practising repeatedly, the movements become familiar and natural so that the performance is easier in reality.

EXERCISE 7: CREATE A PERFECT MORNING VISUALISATION FOR YOURSELF

1. Write down an area of your life that you want to visualise going well. I am going to use a typical working day in the office for this example. You are going to write down *how you want to feel, and what you want to see and hear* to bring it to life.

2. Describe how alert you feel when you wake up in the morning, excited for the day ahead. Describe *what you want to feel, what you see and hear*.

3. Write down your positive morning routine. *Hear* the sound of the shower, the feeling of your clean clothes, experience a moment of quiet. *Feel* the movement of walking, *see* mental signposts on your journey as you leave home feeling calm, prepared and purposeful.

4. Describe your perfect journey. *See* a free seat on the train or imagine a parking space at work. *Feel* the pleasant feeling of an early morning walk.

5. Write down your best, most productive and positive day at work – doing what you do to the best of your ability. Add any specific details of what you see, hear or feel that tell you this is a brilliant day.

6. Describe the end of the working day and the pleasant and efficient journey home. Add the feeling of contentment on arriving home and a satisfying end to your day.

7. Look over what you have written down and add any details that make this a really compelling and desirable day – you really want this to be an achievable best possible day for you.

8. Now use a voice recorder on your phone or other device to record you speaking this aloud slowly. It needs to be slow enough so that you can imagine it when you listen back to it.

You now have a visualisation recording to listen to before you go to bed. Therapists often make recordings like this for their clients, and this is a simple way for you to try it out for yourself. Some people find it easy to close their eyes and imagine the scenario that they want to create without prompts, but most people like the guidance in a recording. It can really help to play meditative music in the background, as it sets the scene, helping you to breathe more slowly and cutting out other distractions.

A recording like this supports your unconscious mind to override the habit of imagining a negative scenario, by giving it all of the details needed to bring to life *what you want instead*. It gives your mind all of the information to focus on, to help you create *that* reality. The best time to listen to recordings like this are as you fall asleep at night or are able to relax at home. Don't ever listen to this sort of recording when you are driving or need to concentrate, as you may become distracted! You need to listen to the recording for at least two weeks to allow the unconscious mind to update, and the longer you continue for, the more permanent the change is likely to be.

CHAPTER 8

Start to Do Things for Yourself

If until now, you have been constantly putting others first, you probably haven't been doing many of the things you want to do.

One of the most precious commodities we have is time. It's something that's finite and the modern world is full of distractions, so it's all about how carefully we use it. We save time, spend time, give our time and we make time for people and our hobbies. But a lot of my clients have spoken about the feelings of guilt that they have around spending time or money on themselves. They are happy to do things for others and consider the needs of their families, yet they are often left feeling a bit empty, because they don't usually prioritise their own desires. Putting the needs of their spouse, children, parents, siblings, boss or colleagues before their own *all of the time* is not balanced.

One of Omar's great loves is enjoying artisan coffee. He would go out of his way to visit a coffee shop, taking the long way round on his walk, but this would annoy his wife, who couldn't see the point of travelling so far. For Omar, there was something important about supporting a business who cared as much as they did about their craft, and he wanted to be part of that experience. He decided this was a treat that he could afford himself – it was the gift of time doing something he enjoyed, and that it's okay to spend some time or money on yourself or to treat someone. I agree! Once you have taken care of all of your needs, it is a good idea to enjoy some of life's pleasures.

Feelings of Guilt

Guilt is one of those emotions that some people feel deeply, and it tends to be those who think of others before themselves. Perhaps you were brought up around feelings of guilt or it is an emotion that crops up from time to time. Nicola spoke to me about her feelings of guilt she experienced anytime she spent money on herself. She said it felt as though she was taking money away from the family budget, even though she wasn't, and that made her feel guilty. She also had a desire to spoil her daughter with treats from time to time. Nicola explained that money had been scarce when she was a child, despite her parents working all hours. She and her brother were always well cared for, and they never missed out, despite the hardships. Now her mum is retired, and Nicola is in a position to be able to take her out for the day and treat her with gifts. Even though Nicola has provided everything her family needs first, she notices some resistance from her partner about the money she spends on her mother. This creates a feeling of guilt in her, as if she is taking away from her family and giving money away. Through exploring this, she decided to share her feelings about it with her partner. She has now recognised that she has already met all of her financial responsibilities, and that it makes her happy to treat her mother or her daughter. Nicola has decided to continue treating others, without the guilt. For some people, guilt is ever-present. Try this exercise to help. Be aware that more complex situations may require support from a therapist.

EXERCISE 8A:
REDUCING GUILT VISUALISATION*

You can download the template from:
https://zeenatahmedpeto.com/book-bonuses/

1. Alternatively, in your journal or on a sheet of paper, make a list of all of the things you would like to do if you didn't have the feelings of guilt holding you back. Be sure to add things that you want to do for yourself and allocate the amount of time, money, or other resources you would need. E.g. – a day out visiting an exhibition/show/event of your choosing. Write down the monetary cost and the amount of time needed for the day out.

2. Visualise yourself doing the most important thing on your list. Remember to write down what you see, hear and feel as you visualise yourself enjoying the event.

3. Notice when and where the guilt comes in. Pause the visualisation. What is the feeling of guilt saying to you? Write this down.

4. Imagine the feeling of guilt as a shape, with qualities.
   **For example: *The guilt is like a heavy grey cloud moving slowly and casting a shadow over the scene. The feeling of excitement changes to a dense nagging feeling that takes over the feeling of desire.*

5. Imagine that you could transform that image into something lighter.
   For example: Lighten the colour of the cloud, make the shape smaller, watch the cloud disappear into thin air. Keep practising this visualisation. This is just an example. Manipulate the shape any way you can to reduce the potency of the feeling of guilt.

6. Now imagine your visualisation of your day out/event/day for yourself *without that cloud. What do you have instead?* Maybe a different, positive feeling like excitement can come in instead.

7. Describe how this positive feeling appears to you.

    For example: *A multi-coloured rainbow shoots into the frame. As the excitement builds, the colours become more vibrant.*

8. What does this new feeling, for example – excitement, say to you? Write down the encouraging and positive words associated with doing something you really want to do for yourself.

9. Now replay the visualisation of your day out. It could be a film, a series of pictures, words on a page, or thoughts and feelings.

10. Bring in the *positive feeling* (e.g. excitement) and make the image bigger, the scene louder, more intense. Increase the vibrancy, bring in some movement, a happy soundtrack. Notice how much more compelling and exciting it feels, and that any negative feelings can be dwarfed by the positives. They might even shrink or disappear entirely, replaced by the positive feeling.

11. When your positive feeling is at a peak, squeeze your thumb and middle finger together to form an *anchor*. As you practise this, and press your thumb and middle finger together, it can form a 'switch' which helps bring on the positive feelings associated with it.

12. Each time you practise your visualisation, press the anchor (tips of your thumb and middle finger) at the *peak* of your positive feeling. This forms a strong association.

13. Keep practising every day. After a few days, you can bring on the associated peak positive feeling, by simply pressing your anchor.

A Note on Visualisation

*Visualisation is a useful process which can aid our thinking, especially if you are a highly 'visual person'. A visual person is someone who can think of pictures in their heads without trying. If you have a strong visual sense, you probably like how things look, or can tell if they don't look right. You might notice the appearance of a place before the ambience or the soundscape. If this resonates, you will probably enjoy the exercise shown above. If, however, you don't really see pictures in your head or find it hard to imagine things, this exercise might be harder for you. It may be that feelings, sounds, or rational thoughts are what you notice first and are how you prefer to think or learn. If you find visualising difficult, you could try reframing your thoughts about feelings of guilt (see Chapter 5, Exercise 5: Reframing Negative Thoughts).

**This is an example for illustrative purposes. Everyone's feelings will *appear* differently. It may not appear at all, as visualising uses the ability to see in your mind's eye. It may be that for you, it's feelings or a series of words, phrases or thoughts that you notice.

This exercise is simply showing how to manipulate the qualities and change them into something more comfortable. Generally, increasing the size and shape of something makes a feeling stronger and vice versa, but this is not always the case. Each visualisation should be specific to you, so play around with the image or feeling to make it just right.

This is a great exercise to explore in your journal. Once you have an idea of the images, words and feelings, you can practise visualising your day out with the new feelings of excitement regularly.

A Date with Yourself

Make an appointment with yourself for your day out (or activity of your choosing) and start making the arrangements to make it happen. You might enjoy time alone doing the thing you love, but it could also be fun to enjoy this hobby with other enthusiasts. As much as possible, try to ensure that the time you carve out for yourself is earmarked as 'sacred' time. For many people, their own enjoyment is the thing that gets left off the timetable when there are time pressures. As we know, this is not good for us in the long run, so in the interests of filling our cup and creating balance, try to keep your date with yourself.

A Date with Others

One of the best ways to start a new hobby is to find a group of like-minded people to do it with. It can also be motivating, especially if you are planning to go to the gym after a long day's work, for example. If you know you are going to meet a friend or personal trainer there, it can make it easier to stick to your plans. When you are committed to a hobby with someone else, you are more likely to go along, as there are others waiting for you. It's also a great way to meet new people and share your passion and excitement with others who feel like you do.

Keeping Your Dates

Work or family requests can crop up at the last minute, and you might find yourself reluctantly letting go of your time and hobby, to do the thing that's been asked of you. If the feeling of guilt crops up again, try the exercise above. Recognise the qualities of the guilt and then change them to something more manageable. Keep transforming the qualities to something more comfortable, until the guilt reduces or even disappears.

The space left behind can allow new positive feelings to come in, like feelings of excitement. Remember the multi-coloured rainbow shooting into the frame? (Exercise 8a: Reducing Guilt Visualisation). However, you recognise that positive feeling, thought, picture or word, manipulate it in whichever way you have to, to allow that to grow and take up more of the frame.

As the feelings of guilt around doing things for yourself start to dissipate, make a pledge to start doing one or two of the things on your list regularly over the coming months. Having plans in your diary can change the dynamics of your week or months ahead, increasing your engagement and excitement.

What's Going Well?

When you are starting to do things for yourself, it's important to do the inner work, too. Start off by really understanding what is working well in your life. This could be in the form of journaling or thinking about your life while walking outside in nature. Start with all of the positives you can think of and resist the temptation to become bogged down in negatives. I find it's always useful to commit your thoughts to paper, even if you analyse them mentally first. This is because our minds are so dynamic, that thoughts and feelings change regularly, progress and move on. It can be very helpful to have a written record of your thoughts, as you can reflect on your ideas at a later date. Many of my clients are surprised when I relay their words back to them from earlier sessions. It's as though they can't believe they used to think those outdated thoughts! For many people, the process of self-discovery is a one-person job; they want to explore their inner world by themselves, guided by ideas or resources like this book. If you find it hard to do this work yourself, you could supplement it with talking therapy of your choosing. Working with an experienced therapist can help you work out what you really want in life and your next steps.

Zoe knew she was unhappy carrying on living the way she had been. She started therapy, which gave her a place to think aloud and understand her own thoughts, without the noise of everyone else's needs shouting out at her, and their beliefs clouding her judgement. As a person who had always prided herself on being considerate to others, she needed the space to be able to hear her own voice. It did not take long for her to be able to tune in and listen to what was being whispered inside.

The Five Wells by Jenny Mosley

One of the simplest and most transformative models I came across early in my teaching career was the work of Jenny Mosley. (Mosley. J, www.circle-time.co.uk). She worked with school leaders to improve self-esteem and positive relationships in school communities. The model which I learnt back then is something I still think about to this day, because it was shared to improve the well-being of teachers. Jenny explained that in her model there are five wells: physical, emotional, intellectual, spiritual and creative. Each of the wells is deep and can be drawn upon whenever you need a boost of that energy. But they can also become empty and need refilling regularly to maintain balance across your life. As a young teacher, like my peers, I was in the habit of working very hard during the term and then collapsing in exhaustion as soon as it was the holidays. Some of my peers would become sick as soon as it was half-term, leaving their plans to go awry, scrambling to get better in time for the back-to-school rush. All of our 'fun activities' were bunched up in the holidays, with nothing spread over the term. If we had managed to inject some down-time and time for hobbies into our school term, it might have been a key to improving our work-life balance. That would have helped to ensure that we were filling our physical, emotional, intellectual, spiritual and creative wells over the weeks and months, not as isolated incidents.

EXERCISE 8B: HOW TO USE THE FIVE WELLS

You can download the blank template from: https://zeenatahmedpeto.com/book-bonuses/

Alternatively, write down the headings of the five wells in columns in your journal or on a sheet of paper. Under each heading list all of the activities you do on a weekly basis which fit under those headings. Rate yourself from 0 to 5 for each column, 0 being the lowest and 5 being the highest.

1.   Which of those wells is most full?

2.   Which well needs filling?

3.   Work out activities you could do to explore a dry and empty well. As you fill your columns, you will find that some activities fill more than one well. For example, if you meet a friend for a walk to talk about your ideas for a project, you could be filling the physical, emotional, and intellectual wells at the same time.

Here's an example:

Exercise 8b: The Five Wells example

Well / Activity	Physical	Emotional	Intellectual	Spiritual	Creative
Current Activities:	Walking. Going for a run.	Discussing the day's events at the dinner table.	Reading at work. Writing reports. Watching news items. Non-fiction books.	Walking in nature. Quiet reflection.	
Activities I could do:	Join a walking group. Go to an organised running event.	Meet friends regularly. Join a cause that you care about.	Listen to a podcast or. audiobook. Join a book club.	A meditation practice. Silent prayer.	Sketching. Creative writing. Use creativity with a sense of style.

Filling your wells is a way to replenish your joy and excitement in life. By auditing your wells, you can find out what is missing and take steps to redress that balance. It is especially useful when you are at a time of rethinking your life or are at a crossroads because you are actively creating what you want more of. You can create more balance and fulfilment across your life.

Creating a Sense of Excitement in Your Life

It helps us to have things to look forward to as the brain will start simulating scenarios and trying out ideas. If you book to meet a friend to go to an exhibition and have lunch, you will probably have an idea of what to see and where to meet. Before you have even booked the date, you are imagining what it would be like to do that enjoyable thing. When we are preoccupied with the stresses and strains of work and relationships, doing nice things for ourselves can be the last thing we think of. So this is a reminder to fill your cup.

Omar loves being creative in his work. He noticed that his creative well was completely empty, which was adding to his lack of motivation in life. At the time, he was struggling with building and running a successful business in hospitality. His flair and passion for design was the thing that made his heart sing, so he thought about how to bring more of that into his life. To help him, he started mentoring other people, engaging in their creativity, injecting his passion and expertise. This was really fulfilling for Omar, and it was a bridge that carried him from a dark place emotionally, back into the thing he loves best: his work. Looking at his character strengths showed that 'appreciation of beauty and excellence' was one of his top strengths. For him, watching someone create something beautiful with passion, spoke deeply to him. Helping his colleagues hone their craft brought him immense pleasure, and so he was able to bring himself back to a positive mindset, achieving an equilibrium.

Choose Where You Spend Your Energy

When you are starting to do things for yourself and making your personal happiness a priority, you will inevitably rethink where you spend your time. This could involve rethinking who you spend your time with. It could mean working out who you feel aligned with and moving away from those who no longer resonate with you. This could be individuals or a group of people. Rather than continuing a relationship out of habit or duty, consider the impact of maintaining the same level of contact in that relationship. Is it really making you happy enough to continue prioritising at this stage of your life? What changes can you make to help you improve the quality of your relationship? Is this relationship important enough to you to make those changes?

Pledge to Make Your Changes

It is very possible to transform the quality of a relationship when you are changing from within. When you work on yourself and figure out who you are and what makes you feel alive and content when all is well in your world, you will inevitably change.

If those changes continue to spread throughout your life, you will start to have a knock-on effect on those around you, especially the people you spend the most time with. They, in turn, will change. It's inevitable. They *cannot not* change. Change comes from within, and it spreads outward. If you are desperate to improve your life, you can. But it has to come from within. Seek out the support you need, harness a positive mindset and try the tips in this book to help you. It starts with a decision, and that can only come from you.

Here are a set of actions you can take to increase your positive self-regard and self-esteem over time. You could pick the one which seems easiest first, or the one which feels like it will make the biggest impact.

EXERCISE 8C:
PRACTISE SELF-LOVE

You can download this exercise from:
https://zeenatahmedpeto.com/book-bonuses/

1. Write down *positive attributes* about your character and turn them into affirmations*. E.g. Turn 'I am a kind person' into the affirmation: 'I am a kind and compassionate person and I choose to love *myself* now.'

   *Please note that affirmations usually start with 'I' or 'I am'. The present tense is important because it helps the brain to imagine that it is already true, so it is easier to accept. Focus on the positive – what you do want, not what you don't want.

2. Write down positive *physical* attributes about yourself and turn them into compliments. E.g. Turn 'I am happy with my body' into 'I am grateful for my body, which allows me to enjoy life in so many ways.'

3. Say these affirmations aloud to yourself as you brush your teeth every morning, whilst looking in the mirror. You could write them on Post-it notes and stick them up as a reminder. NB: Your affirmations should be in the first person and in the present tense (I am…) and you may not *yet* believe them. They are *aspirational* thoughts.

4. Write down any compliments friends or colleagues say to you.

Keep them in a box with any cards, letters and emails with kind messages in. This will form a bank of positive messages you can read anytime you need a boost.

5. Accept compliments from other people, rather than batting them away. Rather than saying 'Oh, this old thing?' practise saying 'Thank you.' and leave it at that.

6. Catch the way you are talking about yourself. Think of how you would talk about a dear friend and speak about yourself with the same respect and kindness. How you talk about yourself tells the world how you want to be spoken to and treated.

7. Write down anything which you need to forgive yourself for. Understand what you did or didn't do and why. Work out if you need to take some action to resolve the issue or make some form of reparation. Resolve to forgive yourself so that you can be free of this feeling.

8. Do small things for yourself each day that bring you joy.

9. Pledge to make amends with anything in your life that needs resolving and make a start.

10. Think about your ideal life and how you would feel if that were a reality.

11. Surround yourself with people who share your values. Limit the time you spend with people who bring you down or make you question your path.

12. Be wary of what you consume so that you watch, read and engage with positive influences which help you maintain the good feelings you have about yourself.

CHAPTER 9

You Can't Make
Someone Else Happy

You are reading this book because you want to examine your life, work out what's going well and what you want to change. We go through phases of exploring and maintaining and if you are reading this book, it would seem that you are currently seeking to explore.

The thing is, you can't make other people in your life explore if they don't want to. By all means, you can encourage them and lead by example, with the understanding that they have to find their own path. You can drop hints, lend books, share articles and have conversations, but ultimately, it's up to them to find what resonates, if and when they are ready. They must come to their own realisation that they want to make changes, and it is also up to them how they do that. When we are so wowed by our own transformations, we can become evangelical about whatever has helped us. It can be hard to remember that what has worked for us may not work for them. There are so many options out there, from sport to creative outlets to talking therapies, that there is no telling what will help a person who is seeking to explore. Each person must seek and find out what resonates with them and then take steps on their own path. Hopefully, it will unravel as it should. You can certainly be a cheerleader and encourage your loved ones along their route, but don't expect that everyone you speak to will do the same thing as you.

Change Can be Threatening

Sometimes when we are changing, and a significant other can see that, it can feel threatening. It can feel like a rejection, as we are choosing to be different to how we once were. The other person can feel a lot of pressure to also start changing, and this can cause resistance and friction.

David, whom I have talked about previously, wanted to make changes himself and he also really wanted to help his wife Ellen. She had seemed stuck and unhappy for a number of years.

David's wife was so fearful every time he tried to mention any kind of self-help tools. She was in denial that anything was wrong, although they were often bickering or worse still, hardly speaking. Their lives had become quite separate, and they really only spoke about logistics and about the other members of their families – their adult children or elderly parents. While Ellen was in denial, David was busy working on making changes to himself. He was talking to a therapist and was actively seeking answers to the questions which had plagued him for years. He started playing squash once a week, arranged to go hiking on some weekends, and made dates to meet up with friends more often. For years he had put things off as they were inconvenient to fit around family life. David realised that he had lost a lot of connections along the way because he hadn't nurtured them. Friends had moved on and when an old friend died suddenly, he grasped the fact that time was rushing on, and that this time would not last forever. He felt an urgency to act now and to make the most of his health and this stage of his life, while he was well enough to be active, and had the means to pay for things he wanted to do. David was making plans for the next stage of his life, with or without Ellen as a part of it. Watching him transform before her eyes was difficult for her. Despite David urging Ellen to try talking to a professional, he understood that she was on her own journey, and he wanted to carry on with his own one, too. He came to accept that they were going at their own speeds and might end up moving in different directions.

A Catalyst to Change

Sometimes there is a catalyst – an event or a turning point that changes the landscape of a relationship. It can be a slow process which takes time – like the erosion of soil beneath a building. Sometimes the other person makes the decision for us, creating a sense of urgency to face the problem head-on. This can be when we have to face the 'elephant in the room' and start communicating more openly.

Whatever the reason, when the time for change comes upon us, it's our time to step up. We have a choice about how to respond and whether to go along with things or ask for what we need. People can't help how they feel, but they can be considerate about how they behave when they are sharing those feelings. Sometimes one person is not aware of how the other person's feelings have changed, or the extent of the change. They may have been burying their head in the sand or have genuinely missed the clues along the way. Either way, using compassion to allow them to catch up and come to a place of acceptance can make a huge difference to all concerned.

Zoe had always felt that her hand was forced. At the time, when her marriage finally broke down, it seemed that the decision came out of the blue for her. In that moment, she was blindsided – she just didn't see it coming. She knew deep down that things were not right and that she should not feel so unhappy, every day in her relationship, and yet, she was unable to see any way of making it better. If only Tom would spend more time at home, and they talked like they used to. Zoe recalled spending a lot of her energy and time trying her best to do what she thought he wanted.

Over time, her social life came to revolve around his friends and activities. On top of that, she was often trying to placate her parents' wishes. At times, she could see that she was growing distant from her own friends, and it felt uncomfortable choosing to spend so much time with this new group. It was fun, and she did form strong bonds with Tom's friends, but she later regretted letting go of so much of herself. Little by little, she felt she lost part of her identity. Zoe continued to do whatever she could to make Tom happy, but to no avail. In truth, he had checked out long ago and she had not been able to see and accept that fact. She realised that while she was trying to please everyone around her, she had forgotten to please herself. It was too painful to acknowledge and so she carried on until the day it all changed-when he ended the relationship. No more guessing, no more pretending. It was over.

Once the dust had settled, and she started to accept that the relationship was finished, they could finally go their separate ways and start afresh. Looking back, Zoe describes the heartbreak as both the hardest thing she had ever been through, and the best thing that could've happened. She was not strong enough at the time to make the changes necessary and she needed Tom to make a clear decision and declare the chapter closed, rather than them limping on for eternity.

Change Can Help Others Too

If you are truly unhappy, by changing things, you are helping yourself and the other people in your life in the long run. It may not seem like it at the time, but by listening to your higher self and really tapping into your gut feeling, you can hear your inner voice. It might be whispering very quietly, hoping to be heard, or it may already be shouting at you. You know what you really want deep down. It's just that there are difficult choices and decisions to make along the way that have consequences for other people and other parts of your life. Regardless, even if you know what you really want, it doesn't make any difference unless you pay attention to it and take action, and those actions will most likely have knock-on effects for years to come. The words and tone of voice you use, and the way you conduct yourself will be part of your collective journey. Think about how you want to be perceived or how your actions will be received. This will help you create a plan for moving forward and ensure that you're prepared so you can make the necessary changes in the kindest possible way for all concerned.

If you are unhappy in your relationship, and you are ending it, your partner will thank you for the decision you're making now in the future. It might not feel like it at the time, but there is no point staying in a relationship if one person doesn't want to be there. You deserve to be loved wholeheartedly, and so do they. You both deserve to be free to love wholeheartedly, too.

There will be people you know who have ended relationships and are so much happier than when they were in it. With the benefit of hindsight, Zoe is so grateful that her relationship with Tom ended. She couldn't have known that at the time, but she can now see that it was the best thing that could've happened. Tom is also happy in his life, and the choices they made set them both free to start again. It gave them the freedom to realise that their relationship was no longer as it once was, and that they could be happy with new people.

It may be that you have tried to make others happy all of your life. This could be significant people like your parents or partner, for example. Even though you've tried, it hasn't worked, because whatever you do, you can't create someone else's happiness for them. This is true despite your best efforts over a significant amount of time. Whatever you have said or done, you just haven't been able to do it. It may feel that despite the appeasing, people-pleasing and bending over backwards, it hasn't worked! This comes back to the point that it is not your responsibility to make others happy. Of course, when we love someone, we want the best for them, and we can do our best to create a loving home and a positive relationship. But often, when someone is chronically dissatisfied, this is to do with their outlook on life and how they see the world. It can become a habit to complain or generally have a lack of satisfaction. The good thing about habits, is that they can change, with some effort, which you can point out tactfully. You can also recognise what is a personality trait, what is a habit, and what is possible to change.

Ultimately, you can only do your best to create harmony and happiness, but it is their responsibility, too. They have to decide what it is they want and need, and then make the decision to improve their life.

You Can't Make Someone Else Happy, But You Can Break the News Kindly

Even though your decision to change or end, your relationship might cause hurt to someone else, you can do it kindly. In life in general, it's a good thing to speak kindly. You can lead by example and show respect to your partner, even though you might be talking about very difficult topics. It's also important to be clear and unambiguous. This can be difficult when the *situation itself* is ambiguous. You might not yet know what you want to do, but you might be considering a trial separation, to create a bit of space to think. It is important not to make false promises, as this can lead to further hurt and disappointment. Be honest. It's time to communicate clearly and fairly. Try to make changes in the kindest possible way, setting them up for the future, especially when there are children involved in the relationship. All of this will help you walk away with a clear conscience.

Christos was very considerate when he moved out of the family home. He tried to do it gradually so as to ease the pain, making sure that he moved his belongings out a little at a time. Christos didn't want Eleni to be there when he left, as he knew it was very painful for her. He took care to move things away slowly while she was out, knowing that he was able to mitigate the hurt that these changes were causing her. Christos was critically aware of the effect of the separation on their daughter, so for several months he came home in time for bath and bedtime to maintain their regular family routine.

Molly and Stuart co-parented their son Rory from when he was a toddler to being an adult, and have always maintained a good working relationship, for the sake of their son. Even though their marriage came to an end, and they both remarried, they placed their child at the centre and worked everything around his welfare. It has been a successful example of how to bring up a child when a relationship breaks down. Even though they ended their relationship, Molly and Stuart have managed to maintain a mutual respect and positive regard for each other. They could not be happy together, but they have managed to be happy for each other, while being happy apart.

You can't make someone else happy. It's time to start with you.

The following exercise can help you shed light on how you feel about yourself at the present moment. The scores will help you see the areas where you need to focus your attention.

EXERCISE 9:
KNOW, LIKE AND LOVE

You can download the template from:
https://zeenatahmedpeto.com/book-bonuses/

1. Alternatively, take a sheet of paper or start a new page in your journal.

    Rate yourself out of 10 for the following questions, with 10 being the highest and 1 being the lowest.

2.   a. How much do you know yourself? Score out of 10

    b. How much do you like yourself? Score out of 10

    c. How much do you love yourself? Score out of 10

3.   Write for 15 minutes about the scores you gave for a, b and c.

It is possible to know yourself but not like or love yourself or love yourself but not like yourself. Reflect on your answers and think about how this impacts you.

4.   What do you need to do to be the best version of yourself?

5.   What do you pledge to do now to increase your self-esteem and boundaries bit by bit?

CHAPTER 10

You Can Explore Your Possible Next Steps

There are interim steps you can take before jumping in (or jumping out) headfirst into a new phase of your life. Taking things slowly will give you the time to test out ideas and see how you feel and how your decisions are taken by significant others around you. Ending a relationship might be the ultimate result, but prevention is better than cure, so taking your time thinking through your next steps is vital. Being as sure as possible is the best way to avoid buyer's remorse later. It is easier to break something apart than it is to put it back together again.

Changes to Explore

David spent time thinking about where he might live if he moved out. He considered a flat nearer to work, halfway between his office and the family home. This would mean he could see his children easily and claw back some time for himself in the evenings after work. He dreamt about the extra time he would gain, being able to see his friends and go to the gym. The idea of living alone after so many years filled him with a mixture of dread and excitement. The only way he could imagine a new life after breaking up, was to try on the ideas in his head, first, as they felt so alien. To make it more realistic, he did his sums and worked out how he would support his family, and ensure that his wife was financially secure, whilst starting afresh.

In the meantime, before he made any decision on his marriage, David considered changing jobs. Maybe this would be the change he was looking for? He also thought about studying, starting a sideline business, or doing something creative to satisfy his thirst for knowledge and desire for change.

Having been in a period of limbo for several years had meant that lots of decisions about their home had not been made, adding to their feelings of frustration. David and Ellen agreed to declutter their home of unused and outgrown belongings. They rearranged their furniture, reorganized their rooms to ensure they were making the best use of their space for their family, and completed some outstanding home repairs. All of these changes to their home environment improved their overall sense of well-being and meant that they started to communicate more freely. Whatever happened, he wanted to know that he had explored every avenue, leaving behind him the least damage, and that he was going into the next phase of his life, ready to live life to the full.

Living Apart as an Interim Step

When Sam and Lisa's relationship faced an uncertain future, Sam rented a flat as an interim step. This bought them time while he and Lisa worked out what they would do next. With two young children, they were keen to keep the stability and family routines going. Sam would come home every evening after work and spend time with the family, leaving after the children's bedtime. The boys were used to their dad leaving for work before they got up for school, which eased the pressure of any unwanted questions. By agreeing from the start to try to create as little impact on the family as possible, they were forced to speak to each other with respect and kindness. This gave them the opportunity to work through their problems in marriage counselling, while maintaining their calm exterior at home. The children would attend activities or visit grandparents on the weekends, which gave the couple time to work on their relationship. After six months, the lease of the flat was up for renewal. Sam didn't renew it and moved back into the family home. The couple decided that what they had together was too much to lose, so they continued with their counselling and managed to get over their hurdles and stay together.

Moving Out to Find Yourself

Christos, on the other hand, moved out when he felt he had no other choice. Living together was proving toxic for his relationship, and he wanted to shield himself, and more importantly, his daughter from that experience. He didn't like the person he was becoming whilst being around his wife, Eleni. Their relationship was stifling and was bringing out the worst in him. He knew her mental health was suffering, and he felt the kindest thing he could do was to remove himself from the vicinity and offer his support from further away.

Moving out into his own space was a breath of fresh air. It gave Christos his own place with distance between him and Eleni and allowed things to settle. He felt a sense of peace and the space, both metaphorical and physical, and living without all of their belongings and memories in their home afforded him a bit more perspective. Even though he was renting a faceless apartment, the sense of relief he felt was overwhelming and immediate. He chose not to go and stay with his family, as he realised that his relationships with them was part of his problem. People had been crossing his boundaries for years, and it all stemmed from the beliefs formed in his early life within his childhood home. He had been encouraged to be kind to others and put them first, and this he did for years at the cost of his own happiness. He had not yet learnt how to be kind to himself.

Moving out gave Christos the space to relax and to breathe, without fear of an argument breaking out. He was able to give his system the chance to calm down after the continual feeling of adrenaline surging through his body for so long. He hadn't appreciated how on edge he had been feeling. Being in his own space meant that he was much calmer when he and Eleni spoke, so they were able to have more productive conversations more often. During this time, he maintained regular contact with his daughter, which took a huge amount of effort. A lot of his time in therapy was spent working out how to negotiate with his partner who was not willing to compromise and who sometimes withheld access to seeing their child.

Christos spent time re-evaluating his life and what he wanted from it and how he wanted to live. Over time, he came to realise he couldn't go back to living together and being in this relationship in the same way, until major things changed.

When Living Together is Unsafe

For some people, a marriage or relationship can turn very sour and be a dangerous place to remain. In this situation, it is imperative to ensure your safety and the safety of any children first. By seeking legal advice, you can find out what your rights are and glean advice on the best way to resolve the situation. It may be that one of you should move out until the immediate crisis is over.

Eva and Max had met online, and they moved in together prematurely due to the lockdown rules during the pandemic. At first, things were going well, but they knew this was an unusual situation. Eva didn't want to be alone during lockdown. Her family lived in Croatia, and she knew it would be months before she could visit them again. They had not yet met each other's family or friends, but Max moved into her flat so they would not be alone at such an unusual time. Over the coming months, the feelings of isolation from the rest of the world grew, and this was coupled with the suffocation of working and living in a small flat. Over time, Max had started to show his temper, and Eva started to feel uncomfortable about living together. She had become so used to being alone with him that she had lost her confidence and could no longer differentiate what was normal or unusual. She had begun to tolerate more and more coercive and violent behaviour.

As soon as the lockdown rules were relaxed, Eva was able to take up the offer of staying with friends. Talking to Max from her friend's flat allowed her to have the courage to speak out. She told him she was ending the relationship and asked him to move out, to avoid more conflict and heartache. Eva spent time in therapy, which helped her come to terms with what she had been through and how she had allowed the crossing of so many of her boundaries.

Embracing Your New Life

In the case of Barbara, she decided that she wanted a divorce after a major betrayal led to the breakdown of her marriage. When the full extent of the deception was revealed, she was numb with shock. Even though she made the decision to sell the family home and downsize, she was not able to start the process for a year. She decided to take care of herself and do nice things every day until she felt ready. She described this as looking after herself. She was finally putting her needs before that of her husband, her children and her work. She was taking care of herself for the first time. During the time Barbara was healing from the shock, she felt that she had little attachment to the house which had been their family home for 30 years. Some of the memories seemed tarnished now, and so she decided to move on and find a new place of her own. Her adult children were all settled, and now that she had given herself time to come to terms with her change in circumstances, she was ready to move into the next phase of her life. She was starting to feel excited about what she could create for herself for the first time in years.

Seeking Legal Support and Mediation

The legal ramifications of changing or breaking a contract are outside of the remit this book, but it's important to educate yourself in this area. Seek legal advice and consider mediation if you are unable to stay on good speaking terms. This is especially important when children are involved. Mediation services are provided by specialists with legal backgrounds in family law and can provide support for couples and their children. Working with a mediator can keep costs down, which can spiral out of control if the process is an arduous one. You can find out more about mediation at the Citizens Advice Bureau online (https://www.citizensadvice.org.uk/).

EXERCISE 10:
YOUR POSSIBLE NEXT STEPS

You can download the template from:
https://zeenatahmedpeto.com/book-bonuses/

Alternatively, use a page in your journal or a piece of paper to consider your next steps.

1. Which area do you want to explore?

2. What do you already know?

3. What do you need to find out?

4. How will you find out this information?

5. Who do you know who can help you?

6. List your first 10 actions in order.

7. Decide which of the actions you want to do first – the easy ones or the difficult ones.

8. Plan time to take the actions and pledge the date you will start.

CHAPTER 11

You Can Love Yourself and Grow Unconditional Positive Self-Regard

This is the key message I want you to take away at the end of this book.

The definition of self-esteem in the Oxford English dictionary is: Self-esteem, n. Good opinion of oneself; high self-regard; confidence in one's own worth or abilities (https://www.oed.com/, 2023).

When self-esteem is high and a person has unconditional positive self-regard, they can foster a deep love and respect for themselves. I use the analogy of the 'internal pot of gold' to describe self-esteem in a visual way, as described by Professor Simon Baron-Cohen (Baron-Cohen. S, Zero Degrees of Empathy, 2012).

For some of us, we grew up in a home where we felt secure and loved, and we were confident in our connection and attachment to our primary caregivers. That starts us off in life with high levels of self-esteem as young children. This is obviously not the case for everyone, depending on their circumstances. Fortunately, the pot of gold is not static. In fact, it can be topped up at any time. I usually describe it as a pot of liquid gold, or golden honey, shiny and viscous. When we are adults, we can tap into that image of a pot of gold and the feeling of self-esteem. We can measure it on any given day and notice how emotionally strong we feel. If you were to take a reading at this moment, I wonder what your number out of ten would be, with ten being the highest? Make a mental note of this number and check in with yourself from time to time.

When things are going well, the pot is full, and we feel resilient and capable. We keep the pot topped up by spending time with people who make us feel good, because they love us for who we truly are.

It's the unconditional nature of this connection which fills it up and can keep us feeling like we can conquer the world. We also keep it topped up by doing the things that we love that bring us joy, connection, and a sense of purpose. When we have high self-esteem and unconditional positive self-regard, it is *easy* to have healthy boundaries and be kind to ourselves; because we value ourselves.

We know that loving ourselves is beneficial to everyone, because this confidence exudes out of us and positively impacts those around us. We all know how good it feels to be around someone who is secure in themselves and has a quiet confidence about them. They can be loving and warm towards others, but they don't take any nonsense.

Our self-esteem can, of course, be eroded over time or can become depleted when we are challenged or emotionally exhausted. It is not something we should take for granted and we should continue to pay attention and fill it up regularly.

The Importance of Self-Care

When we are unhappy and are trying everything we can to solve the problems that plague us, it can be easy to stop taking care of ourselves. Self-care is an essential part of having a healthy and fulfilling life, but it takes time, effort, and will to make it happen and when we are at an impasse or crisis point, we need self-care more than ever.

Self-care means different things to different people, so I urge you to work out what the essential elements of self-care are for you. What do you absolutely *need* to help you stay balanced and feeling okay? They could be simple things like a cup of tea or coffee in the morning, a comfortable sleep, or a short walk each day. Consider all of the elements of your life and the parts which give you a feeling of comfort, peace, or joy. This can help you find out what will bring you that element of self-care. List your top five or so ideas and then find ways to incorporate a few of them into your week. You might decide to focus on one or to scatter a few across your week ahead. Block out time in your calendar, add reminders or timers to your phone to keep you on track. Pledge to take the time to do what it takes to give you that time for your well-being.

EXERCISE 11:
COMPILE YOUR OWN EXERCISES

You can download the template from:
https://zeenatahmedpeto.com/book-bonuses/

Now that you have tried some of the exercises in this book, you can create your own tailor-made list. Here are some suggestions:

1. Take some physical exercise each day. A daily walk during daylight hours is beneficial for all-around health and well-being.

2. Check which of your wells could do with a top-up (see Chapter 8).

3. Visualise your pot of gold filling up while you do activities which fill your cup and nourish your soul.

4. Write down positive affirmations and say them aloud in the mirror. Compliment yourself whilst looking in the mirror.

5. Talk about yourself as you would a dear friend. Show others how you want to be spoken to and treated.

6. Meditate with guided meditations, with gentle music, or simply spend a few minutes focusing on your breath and becoming still for a few minutes.

7. Spend time in nature and visualise yourself growing roots into the ground, which connect with the roots of nearby trees. Feel yourself being supported by the earth beneath you.

8. Pledge to spend time with the people who you love to be around. We are the company we keep, so create opportunities to enhance emotional connections and fun!

If you feel good about yourself and you value yourself, other good things will follow and the positive feeling will flow into other areas of your life. You will open the door to accepting more opportunities for happiness. As you see more good, you receive more good, because you are looking for the good in the world. You will make a better impact on the world as a human.

In Chapter 1, I shared how I came back to health and well-being after being burnt out from stress and illness. This is an image that came to me some years later.

I was on holiday in Northumberland and was walking on the beach at Bamburgh, which is a breathtaking place of natural beauty. The tide had gone out. The vast beach stretched before me as I walked along the shoreline. As I surveyed the landscape, I saw there before me clumps of exposed rocks, covered in seaweed, just like the ones I had imagined all those years ago. The image of my net, full of holes like my immune system at the time, letting everything through, followed. And as I stood there, it dawned on me: all those years had passed, and now my disease didn't look like that to me anymore. I knew that it was well managed with medicine and lifestyle, and I was the happiest I had ever been. The rocks in the seabed changed in my mind's eye; they were much smaller, and were no longer dark, but iridescent and psychedelic colours! The net was strong and robust, repaired with my heightened self-love and high self-esteem. I realised that when the tide came in, the rocks were completely hidden under the depths, but when they were exposed they served as a reminder to me-to take care of myself and honour myself. Being too kind was a thing of the past. I had learnt to be kind to myself, too.

In this book, I have shared the stories of many past clients who have taught me so much about my work. Even though they are all very different and have distinct desires and outcomes, I could see a common thread running through them. I found that all of them reported that they felt better about themselves than they had in years. They all had a new optimism and a sense of agency, because they had each listened to their inner voice. By listening to that voice coming from the unconscious, and giving themselves somewhere to *express* that voice, they were acting upon it and honouring themselves.

By working on their self-esteem, they improved their boundaries... and vice versa. They created a virtuous circle of improvement while making a positive impact on those around them. With their personal empowerment, they were modelling how to 'get their stuff together' and there was a marked difference in their levels of contentment and self-confidence, which is both attractive and infectious! People like being around other people like this, because it makes them feel more confident too. By saying this is what I want, and this is who I am, they invited their significant others to see them with fresh eyes. They were ready to step into their power and be seen, heard, and honoured. I hope this book will help you take the steps you need to do that, too.

CHAPTER 12

Bonus Exercises

EXERCISE 12A:
SELF-ACCEPTANCE AND THOUGHT RELEASE AND LET GO

You can download the template from:

https://zeenatahmedpeto.com/book-bonuses/

Alternatively, use your journal or paper.

1. Choose a problem to work on. Decide to work on that problem *by accepting that it is there*, and that you want to let it go. Give the problem a label. E.g. If I am angry about a decision taken by my boss, my label might be 'angry with my boss'. Write down the label here: _____

2. Complete this sentence* 'Even though I *(have x problem)*, I deeply and completely love and accept myself.' E.g. *Even though I feel angry with my boss, I deeply and completely love and accept myself.*

3. Now say this sentence out loud 3 times. This is a powerful and freeing statement and can create shifts in your mindset. It declares whatever else is going on, I am okay with myself.

4. Now decide to let that thought go. Write down for 5 minutes about your feelings (which you labelled) and follow the steps for Thought Release and Let Go (Exercise 12b)

EXERCISE 12B:
THOUGHT RELEASE AND LET GO

You can download the template from:
https://zeenatahmedpeto.com/book-bonuses/

You will need some plain paper, an ink pen, a bowl of water and a sink.

1. Take a sheet of paper and an ink pen.

2. Write down all of the examples of when that thinking pattern or belief was causing your behaviour. Identify that belief and label it. Choose one incident when the feelings were very strong. Think about that incident and pay attention to all of the details. Think about the consequences and how you felt afterwards.

3. Now write down as much detail as you can about the scenes you can remember and how you felt at the end of them.

4. Fill up both sides of the paper with your thoughts. Pour as much emotion as you can into them. Use another sheet of paper if you need to.

5. When you are finished, tell yourself you are going to discard those beliefs. You are letting go of them. They have served you for a reason, but you don't need them anymore.

6. When you are ready to let go of those beliefs, rip up the sheet of paper and put all of the pieces into the bowl of water.**

7. Leave the bowl to sit for an hour.

8. When you see that the ink has been lifted from the page, pour the water into the sink. The ink should have lifted off the paper. Symbolically, it is as if the words have been erased and you are discarding them with the thoughts down the drain.

9. Say out loud 'I am releasing these thoughts.'

Each time you actively seek to let go of an old pattern; you are loosening its grip. Remember to follow it with *'Even though I felt* _____ *I deeply and completely love and accept myself.'*

*This statement is used in EFT (Emotional Freedom Technique) and is spoken in conjunction with tapping on meridian points. You can find a practitioner who can teach you how to do EFT, but simply saying the statement aloud can create shifts in your thinking, too I.

** If it is safe for you to do so, you can also burn the pieces of paper in a bonfire outdoors, which is another symbolic way to release outdated and unhelpful thoughts.

EXERCISE 12C:
HOW TO CREATE A VISION BOARD

You can download the template from:
https://zeenatahmedpeto.com/book-bonuses/

Creating a vision board is an empowering method to bring to life your desires for the future. If you create a vision of what you would like to happen, your mind sets about achieving that for you and bringing that into reality. As we know, many things that we create or achieve start with a single thought that plants the seed in your mind. Your unconscious mind is often looking for ways to bring you closer to that desired outcome. A great way to help you develop this vision is by using images. Your unconscious mind will absorb these ideas and help you bring them to reality. This happens already, but with a little thought, you can create your vision consciously. This exercise can be done digitally or with paper and glue.

1. Spend some time journaling, visualising or talking about how you would like your future to unfold. Consider the time frame – one year in the future, five years, ten years?

2. Search online for pictures that represent what you truly desire for your future in your chosen timeframe.

3. Collect the pictures online and compile them onto a document. You can use a website or app to collate the images onto one screen.

4. Alternatively, you can cut out or print pictures and paste them onto card.

5. Choose positive enticing images and words which stir strong feelings of longing and desire in you. This will be more compelling and enticing for your unconscious mind.

6. When you have completed your vision board, display it somewhere where you will see it regularly. A screensaver on your computer or phone is a good example, or if you have made yours out of card, near your bed or desk.

7. The vision board should be visible so that the ideas can seep into the unconscious subliminally.

REFERENCES

p.14 Hay, L.L. (1984) *You can heal your life*. Carlsbad, CA: Hay House, Inc.

p.12 Roet, B. (1986) *Hypnosis a gateway to better health*. London, England: Weidenfeld and Nicolson.

p.12 Mate, G. and Mate, D. (2023) *Myth of normal: Trauma, illness & healing in a toxic culture*. London, England: Vermillion.

p.15 Ehrmann, M. (1927) *Desiderata*. Available at: https://www.desiderata.com/desiderata.html (Accessed: 30 September 2023).

p.24 Reading, S. (2017) 'Reframing Adversity', in *The self-care revolution*. London: Aster.

p.31 The Mind Tools Content Team. (no date) *The Conscious Competence Ladder*. Available at: https://www.mindtools.com/ah651dp/the-conscious-competence-ladder (Accessed: 30 September 2023).

p.37 BBC Radio 5-Live. (no date) *You, me and the big C: Putting the can in cancer - downloads*. Available at: https://www.bbc.co.uk/programmes/p0608649/episodes/downloads (Accessed: 02 October 2023).

p.29 Cherry, K. (2022) *What is neuroplasticity?* Verywell Mind. Available at: https://www.verywellmind.com/what-is-brain-plasticity-2794886 (Accessed: 30 September 2023).

p.56 Ravindran, D. (2021) in *The pain-free m.* London, England: Vermillion.

p.57 van der Kolk, B.A. (2014) *The body keeps the score.* New York, New York: Viking.

p.61 Limmer, E. (1995) 'Freeing and Healing Your Inner Child', in *The body language of illness.* Spirit Lake, Idaho: Freedom Press.

p.53 Steinhouse, R. (2022) *Secondary gain, behind every behaviour is a positive intention – NLP School.* NLP School. Available at: https://www.nlpschool. com/explaining-the-nlp-presuppositions-behind-every-behaviour-is-a-positive-intention/ (Accessed: 04 October 2023).

p.63 Saurabh (2021) *To thine own self be true 'being true to yourself'.* Quotes Plays. Available at: https://shakespearequotesandplays.com/to-thine-own-self-be-true/ (Accessed: 03 October 2023).

p.78 Ruiz, M. (1997) *The four agreements: A practical guide to personal freedom.* San Rafael, CA: Amber-Allen Publishing.

p.78 Ruiz, M., Ruiz, J., & Mills, J. (2010) *The fifth agreement: A practical guide to self-mastery.* San Rafael, CA: Amber-Allen Publishing.

p.80 Robbins, T. (2023) *Tony Robbins: Where focus goes, energy flows!* [Social media post]. LinkedIn. Available at: https://www.linkedin.com/posts/officialtonyrobbins_where-focus-goes-energy-flows-remember-activity-7078024233280286720-16PC/ (Accessed: 03 October 2023).

p.88 Bernstein, G. (2021) *Super attractor: Methods for manifesting a life beyond your wildest dreams.* Carlsbad, CA: Hay House, Inc.

p.88 Bernstein, G. (2023) *Choose again to shift away from negative thoughts.* gabbybernstein.com. Available at: www.gabbybernstein.com/choose-again/ (Accessed: 04 October 2023).

p.103 *The 24 character strengths*. VIA Institute On Character. (no date) Available at: https://www.viacharacter.org/character-strengths (Accessed: 04 October 2023).

p.103 Seligman, M.E.P. (2003) *Authentic happiness: Using the new positive psychology to realise your potential for lasting fulfilment.* London, England: Nicholas Brealey Publishing.

p.105 Dilts, R. (2003) 'Getting Access to the Unconscious', in *From coach to awakener.* Capitola, California: Meta Publications.

p.108 Haefner, J. (2008) *Mental Rehearsal & Visualization: The secret to improving your game without touching a basketball!*
Welcome to BREAKTHROUGH BASKETBALL. Available at: https://www.breakthroughbasketball.com/mental/visualization.html (Accessed: 04 October 2023).

p.118 Mosley, J. (2023,) Jenny Mosley Education Training and Resources. Available at: https://www.circle-time.co.uk/

p.141 Oxford English Dictionary. (No date) Available at: https://www. oed.com/search/dictionary/?scope=Entries&=self-esteem (Accessed: 05 October 2023).

p.141 Baron-Cohen, S. (2012) *Zero degrees of empathy: A new theory of human cruelty and kindness.* London, England: Penguin Books.

9 781068 647901